THE KGA GROUP ~

HOPE YOU ENJOY READING

ABOUT MY JOURNEY !

Cancer
on the
Brain

Cancer
on the
Brain

One Man's Journey of

Baseball, Business, and

Beating the Odds

Jay Lefevers

EMERALD
BOOK CO.

Published by Emerald Book Company
Austin, TX
www.emeraldbookcompany.com

Distributed by Emerald Book Company

For ordering information or special discounts for bulk purchases, please contact Emerald Book Company at PO Box 91869, Austin, TX 78709, 512.891.6100.

Design and composition by Greenleaf Book Group LLC
Cover design by Greenleaf Book Group LLC

Cataloging-in-Publication data
(Prepared by The Donohue Group, Inc.)
Lefevers, Jay.
   Cancer on the brain : one man's journey of baseball, business, and beating the odds / Jay Lefevers.—1st ed.
     p. : ill. ; cm.
   ISBN: 978-1-937110-24-6
   1. Lefevers, Jay. 2. Cancer—Patients—United States—Biography. 3. Baseball coaches—United States—Biography. 4. Businessmen—United States—Biography. I. Title.

RC265.6.L44 L44 2012
616.994/0092   2012930764

Part of the Tree Neutral® program, which offsets the number of trees consumed in the production and printing of this book by taking proactive steps, such as planting trees in direct proportion to the number of trees used: www.treeneutral.com

Printed in the United States of America on acid-free paper
12 13 14 15 16   10 9 8 7 6 5 4 3 2 1
First Edition

Contents

Acknowledgments vii

The First Game 1

Diagnosis. 5

Irons in the Fire 10

Baseball Season. 16

The New Normal 20

The Proposal 26

Antiques 32

It's Not Brain Surgery (Oh, Wait a Minute . . . Yes It Is). 37

Letting Go. 44

Don't Put the Gown on Without Asking Questions 47

Dealing with It 54

Back to Work. 57

Worth the Risk. 62

The Man in the Plastic Mask 65

Radiation Treatment. 69

The Biker Appraisers 76

The Big Boys of Little League 80

The Metal Plate 88

Baseball the Hard Way 93

Learning from My Players 97

Hanging Tough 102

A Nice Lull in the Action 105

Taking One for the Team. 109

Taking the Time to Enjoy Life. 115

Ya Gotta Have Style 120

Rolling with the Hurricanes. 127

The Chance of a Lifetime 134

Playing for Keeps 141

The Final Out 148

When Man Plans, God Laughs 156

Back to the Doctor's Office 161

ER "Dramedy" 165

The "Big C" 174

Man Hands 180

Deal with It 184

The Nonissue of Commitment 191

You're Very Fortunate 201

Breathing in Paradise 208

Family First 214

Post-op 218

Acknowledgments

My thanks go out to all the professionals in the medical field who, while merely performing their jobs, extended my life, not once but twice. The appearance of their names throughout this book, as a mere "thank you," never seems quite adequate. Medicine can do only as much as the body allows it to do, and as strong as a person may be, it is difficult to overcome any trial and tribulation of life without support. Support from family and friends. My family not only supports me, every day of my life, but also allows me to live with my unique, and sometimes contrarian, point of view. They allow me to take risks, to fail, to say no, and to say yes to far more than I can often handle. For this gift and for putting up with me every day, I thank Lyn, Briana, Adam, and Olivia. Briana is my only biological child and never ceases to amaze me with her zest for life. As this book progressed, she became my co-author. I thank the many baseball players who granted me the honor of being their coach; several of their names are mentioned throughout this book. As I taught them the game of baseball, they taught me about life. To those co-workers and employees with whom I have toiled, I thank you for enhancing my life and my business. I extend a huge thank-you to Mary Catherine (M.C.) Coolidge, a writer in Sarasota, Florida, who helped shape this book. M.C. worked for my company over ten years ago; we have remained friends and colleagues in spite of the distance since she moved to Florida. She is simply the most passionate and inspiring writer I know. I recommend all to read her . . . she will challenge you as a reader and make you think. See her website, www. mccoolidge.com. To my incredible team at Greenleaf Book Group, I thank you for listening to my story, particularly given I announced my visit with one day notice, for refining my tale with your amazing technical support, for the creative design, and for tutoring me throughout the complex maze of publishing. And most important, I thank God for providing challenges in my life and for gifting me the tools to face them. It's up to me to learn *how* to use these tools.

Chapter 1

The First Game

LOOKING OUT OVER THE GREEN BASEBALL DIAMOND, I was filled with great pride in the Yankees. OK, maybe the field wasn't green; rather, it was packed dirt with patches and clumps of brown grass yearning for water, fertilizer, or any form of care. And it wasn't the New York brand of Yankees. It was the Clarendon Yankees, the Little League team that I was coaching for the first time.

We had held our first practice a few months before, on the same dusty field we were now playing on. Beyond the outfield was a bus barn, associated with the adjacent elementary school; the dugouts, lacking any concrete floor, were often mud pits thanks to overwatering by the sprinkler system, which apparently spent more time watering the dugout than the dying clumps of grass portraying an infield.

The reason I began coaching was my stepson. After I married Lyn, my second wife, in 2002, I was determined to be the best husband and father I could be. I was forty-two, and now I had three kids to take care of: my biological daughter, Briana, thirteen, and Lyn's two children, Adam, twelve, and Olivia, eleven, who rounded out an incredible blended family.

I had always been a baseball fan. The sport reeled me in as a player beginning at about age eight, encouraged me to collect hundreds of Topps baseball cards, and had me glued to the TV during every possible professional baseball game I could watch. I played the sport until I was about thirty, in the form of high school baseball, "club" ball in college, intramurals, city leagues, and even fast-pitch softball. Basically, if the sport involved a bat and a ball, I was playing it.

I was also involved in coaching Little League baseball. I had coached Junior/Senior Little League for five consecutive years during my twenties, but I had given up my love of coaching to focus on family as a young father and to focus on meeting the growing demands of my career. Now, almost two decades later, with my new and happily expanded family doing well and my businesses thriving, I felt I finally had the time to rejoin the coaching ranks with an inner-city program known as the Clarendon league, which covered central Phoenix. Adam, my stepson, had grown up in this league since T-ball, and coaching him, along with all of the other thirteen- and fourteen-year-old boys in the league, would be fun and challenging simultaneously. By the end of the season, my first year back in coaching, my Little League baseball team, the "Junior Yankees," had a record of eight wins and seven losses. Not too bad.

I really do believe that when boys participate in group sports like Little League, it's a lot more than an opportunity to just play ball. I think coaches, and the interaction with teammates, can teach the team a lot about life, help them develop coping skills, and hopefully help them transition from boys to young men as they develop camaraderie and confidence. I wanted to teach these things to Adam, and to his teammates.

To me, coaching was a lot like running a business. Through the years, my commercial real estate appraisal company would grow from five to a "team" of twenty employees. After a mere six initial years in the industry, I naively decided to venture out from the security of an employer and open my business, with a partner, in 1992. My partner and I would gradually grow the company for more than eleven years, until he resigned, amicably, in 2004. At the time, the company had about ten employees and operated from an approximately 3,500-square-foot space. In early 2004, the business became a sole proprietorship, and over the next five-year period I would scratch and claw to build the company into a twenty-plus-person operation in over 8,500 square feet. Like coaching, operating a business involved organizing, practicing, motivating, and performing.

Adam stepped up and tapped his bat on the plate. He moved his weight to his back foot, rested his bat on his shoulder, and took the stance we had worked on. He was facing a much larger kid who owned the mound. As he gripped the ball in his right hand, the pitcher glared at the batter, who in this instance was Adam, with no smile, no frown, no emotion. Rather, the message he sent to the batter was, "You don't belong here!" His fastball approached speeds no other Junior pitcher was capable of matching, and his curveball would send batters bailing out of the box as if he were throwing at their heads. I would later come to know the pitcher as Jonathan, or J.T. or Jon, and he would become a big part of my, and my family's, life. I wondered what was circling through Adam's head as he stood to face this pitcher in his first official at bat with our Yankees team. Hell, this kid scared *me*; I'm sure Adam was a little uneasy. Nevertheless, I was excited for Adam and for our team. I felt great.

Yet I couldn't forget the numbness in my right foot.

Chapter 2

Diagnosis

"IT'S A PINCHED NERVE . . . the lateral femoral nerve in your hip," my doctor said after examining me for, oh, all of about five minutes. Sixtyish and a neurologist, he sounded very confident in his diagnosis; after all, he'd already put me through a series of tests—a neurological exam, blood work, a magnetic resonance image (MRI), and an electromyography exam, and now, in our fifth appointment, he'd spent most of the time telling me about his own good health and "incredible" physique for a man his age, and implying that his fitness should be an example for me.

He was, in fact, thin, but he didn't appear overly fit, with gray hair; big, round glasses; and somewhat sun-damaged skin. I wasn't overly inspired by either him or his diagnosis. But, as he went on and on about his own commitment to cycling and running, I scanned the framed diplomas that littered his walls and thought to myself that at least he was seasoned and well credentialed.

I told him that I ran marathons. "At your weight," he told me, "you're putting way too much stress on your knees and feet by running marathon distances."

"At *your* weight?" Did I hear him correctly? My weight had fluctuated only slightly over the years between 190 and 195 pounds, and at five feet eleven inches, in my midforties, I thought I was actually in pretty decent shape to run a marathon. In fact, I'd recently begun training in preparation for my sixth marathon—P.F. Chang's Rock 'n' Roll Arizona Marathon—and was thinking I was looking good, having dropped a couple of extra pounds. I was feeling good, too. I wanted a diagnosis for my foot, not for my weight.

Of course, some people might not call my marathon performances running. When I say I run marathons, I'm talking about running to finish, not running to win or set some kind of time record. In fact, after five marathons, I'd had yet to achieve a time of less than five hours (five hours, eight minutes was my best time). True marathon runners have already finished the race, grabbed a snack, had a rubdown, traveled home, and commenced lounging around, watching the coverage on television, by the time people like me even cross the finish line. For me, my expectations were always to finish the race—which I always did—and, one day in the not-too-distant future, to finally succeed in breaking the five-hour barrier, even if only by a few minutes. That way, I figured, for the rest of my life, when asked what my best marathon time was, I'd be able to reply, "Four-plus."

I blamed my poor performance on my physique. With my broad chest, stumpy legs, and calves as thick around as tree trunks, I wasn't born to run—at least not more than two miles.

My wife, Lyn, asked me once, when I was complaining about my nonrunner's physique, why I ran marathons if my body wasn't built for them. She had a point there. Even though I had to prepare for months on end, train day in and day out, and run till it hurt even to sweat, I was determined to finish. And it took every ounce of focus and determination to keep my body from rebelling. Yet, I was going to finish those marathons, damn it, even if it took me five hours—hell, even if it took me six hours.

Running marathons was just one of the many challenges in life that I have felt compelled to experience . . . and conquer; even if the definition of "conquer" was merely to gasp across the finish line an hour after almost everyone else. Whether I was coaching the baseball team or running my business, my determination, my will, my attitude of fighting alone was something that only my wife and Briana could sense.

The doctor, however, wasn't making any effort to figure me out. He was so wrapped up in his own athletic feats that he was unable to focus on me or my symptoms. This is why I had always avoided doctors. I just couldn't understand how they could get to know me in a few minutes. They were too consumed in their own world. I had tried to avoid going to a doctor about the numbness in my right foot, but at last I decided to give it a try. Several months before, I had started experiencing intermittent tingling in my right big toe, and it gradually became continuous numbness. I'd let it go for a while, but lately the numbness and tingling had migrated throughout my foot.

I prided myself on being a coach who would roll up my sleeves and work, on the field, with my players as hard as I expected them to practice. I would hit off my pitchers, run down fly balls with my outfielders, and run the bases during drills. However, I began noticing the enhanced numbness as my right foot would miss a base or I would trip on a small divot in the field and go barreling into the dirt. I would get up, dust myself off, and continue on. The guys always had a good laugh when I went down, but they assumed it was just because I was "old," as they constantly reminded me.

I had ignored the numbness until I couldn't ignore it any longer, and now here I was, in this office, with the neurologist telling me that I was overweight and that my numbness was only a pinched nerve—"meralgia paresthetica," he called it. "Common throughout the general population," he added. "You're fortunate not to have pain and decreased mobility."

His words were a relief.

A pinched nerve was something I could deal with, and I left his Phoenix office on a sunny day in October 2004 feeling as fortunate as he'd told me I was. I wasn't in pain, I wasn't tripping over myself; a nerve was pinched, my foot was numbed. I did what I always did. I worked through it and continued my training for the marathon, and in January 2005, I ran my sixth marathon, finishing—always finishing—but this time with my all-time-worst numbers: five hours, forty-nine minutes. Sure, my entire right foot was numb throughout the race, but what hurt was that as I neared the finish line, I noticed an elderly man, at least twenty years my senior, slowly creeping up on me from behind.

So, with every ounce of energy I had left, I activated my

tree trunks, one of them numb, into a sprint (OK, maybe it was more like a fast jog) and propelled my body to the finish line. I was worried about one thing and one thing only: No way was I going to be photographed crossing the finish line side by side with a sixty-five-year-old who appeared to be carrying around at least ten more pounds than I was. Luck was with me, and I did finish several paces ahead of him, arriving by myself for my glory shot.

Which didn't feel so glorious to me. Many people get an entire night's sleep in the time I took to finish the race; I felt embarrassed and humiliated by my performance. My goal, remember, was to someday get under five hours, and here I was getting closer to six hours. My race time left me convinced that there wasn't a bone in my body that was meant to run. Maybe I wasn't a marathon man after all.

Chapter 3

Irons in the Fire

MARATHON RUNNING WAS JUST ONE OF my many interests (some people say I have too many of them), but my main
activity since the 1980s had been building my career as a commercial real estate appraiser. By the time my right foot was
giving me trouble in early 2005, I'd been appraising real estate
for twenty-five years, working first in the real estate division
of major banks and small, private appraisal companies in the
greater metropolitan Phoenix area, and then setting up shop
with a business partner in the early 1990s.

By 2004, I'd gone further out on my own, separating my
business and professional interests from my former business
partner, and renaming and rebranding my commercial appraisal
firm Lefevers Viewpoint Group, Inc. After all, assigning a

value to a property certainly relies on the viewpoint of the appraiser. In 2005, my firm, with ten employees, some new and several who'd come with me from the original company, was approaching its thirteenth year of operation, and our revenues were scheduled to eclipse the two-million-dollar mark.

My staff and I always put a lot of thought into company meetings, corporate gifts, and the like, and we worked hard on planning and carrying out our holiday and year-end celebrations. Like any other profession, appraisal work can be too serious all year long. At Lefevers Viewpoint Group, we work hard, often putting in long hours and sometimes missing time with our families to meet deadlines or fulfill a contractual obligation to a client. Once a year, it's a total blast to kick back and see just how foolish and ridiculous we can be. With "big" money and cool gifts at stake, the employees usually laugh hysterically while they wholeheartedly battle it out in our annual employee game show! And, even though five-, ten-, and fifteen-year employee "roasts" are always done in the spirit of good-natured ribbing, it doesn't hurt that I have a fantastic team of good-humored colleagues and co-workers. We have always been a group of "characters"—nicknames abound throughout the organization. A former employee was known as "Pig Pen," only because he created such a dust storm around every assignment, you never knew where the truth lay. A client is known as "Shooter," after the character Shooter McGavin from the movie *Happy Gilmore*. That's probably all I need to say about that scenario! John, one of our top-billing appraisers, described the culture of the company as "collaborative, professional, hard working, and fun, with a lot of humor."

By late spring 2005, Lefevers Viewpoint Group was experiencing steady growth, and my family was healthy and happy. Yet I was plagued with the numbness that had started in my right big toe. By June, the numbness had advanced throughout my entire right leg, and a new symptom, severe muscle spasms, was regularly occurring.

The spasms would begin with a tingling feeling that would progress throughout the entire leg and, scarily, was starting to result in a temporary paralysis of the leg, followed by a spastic twitching of my right foot—leaving me, at least for short periods of time, with the "decreased mobility" the doctor had said I was fortunate not to be experiencing when I saw him the previous fall. Fortunately, the spasms never surfaced when I was driving. However, on several occasions I had to stop walking and stand stock-still, waiting for the crazy twitching of the foot to stop.

Once, after one of my daughter Briana's school choir concerts, we were standing in the school courtyard saying our good-byes to the other families, and Lyn and Briana headed off toward the car, unaware that I was still standing on the curb. I was unable to take a step forward because my right leg was simply "dead." I absolutely could not move, except for the uncontrollable twitching of the foot. There I stood, in the middle of the courtyard, with a spastic foot jerking around at the end of a paralyzed leg and my wife and daughter disappearing out of view. OK, it wasn't that bad—within a few minutes my daughter came running back, saying, "Dad, I'm so sorry! Is it the foot?"

Of course, at the time, without understanding the origin of the spasms, we laughed about how odd I must have looked to everyone else leaving the concert—standing by myself, nodding and waving at people passing by, hoping they didn't notice my twitching foot.

The twitching began to affect me at work. During a business meeting, the spasms commenced at exactly the point when the meeting was being adjourned. I didn't want to give a long explanation or show any weakness, so I chose to sit there with my twitching foot out of sight under the table, creating small talk with the others who were politely attempting to get up from the table and leave the obviously concluded meeting.

My objective was to keep at least a few people at the conference table until the twitching subsided and the feeling returned to my leg, so that I could get up and walk out. Although I received some abrupt comments, such as "I really need to get going," and was subjected to a few odd glares, I was able to entertain at least one colleague long enough to accomplish my goal of regaining control of my leg. Later, as I related the story to my family, I made fun of myself—I laughed at my ridiculous chatter, my random conversation, my rambling efforts to keep people at the table with me. Anything to avoid standing up and revealing my "handicap."

In the midst of our laughter, Lyn asked, "How often does this happen?"

"Well, usually a few times a day . . . at least," I responded hesitantly.

"What will you do if this happens when you're driving?" she continued.

"That could be a problem," I said, with more hesitation.

"*Could* be a problem?"

I had no response to her last question—which was more

a statement. Again, my concerns were mitigated; I was convinced that if there were a serious problem, the specialist I had visited would have diagnosed it. But I certainly had no intention of endangering myself, my family, or any fellow driver. Thereafter, my driving trips became very short: to work and back home.

I was really more intrigued by what my body was doing than by figuring out why. I somehow managed to conveniently disregard any potentially serious condition these symptoms could be pointing to, and instead I just kind of focused on observing when, where, and for how long the tingling, the numbness, the twitching would occur and last—almost marveling at it as though I were a spectator. In fact, I'd sometimes call people into the office and say, "Hey, watch this," like a little kid wanting to show off his bloody, skinned-up knee to his buddies. Maybe it was my way of keeping an emotional distance from what was happening to my body. As the spasms became more frequent and occurred with more regularity at work, I'd sometimes have to ask my colleagues and employees to grab hold of my foot and attempt to stabilize it; sometimes the twitching was so strong and uncontrollable, they were unable to hold the foot steady. Still, I tried to make light of it. I didn't want to let them see that I was really struggling with the unknown origin of my problem.

A few people in my office, though, began to question what was going on, doubting my doctor's diagnosis and prodding me to dig deeper. Jessica, my office manager, asked, "Are you sure this is caused by a pinched nerve? This just doesn't seem normal."

"Seriously," I responded, "you think this is a major problem?"

"Yes!" she exclaimed. "*Something* is going on!"

I brushed off her concerns for the time being, but they caused me again to second-guess my physician's diagnosis.

Normal or not, I wasn't going to let anything get in the way of my work, my family, or my baseball team.

Chapter 4
Baseball Season

DURING LITTLE LEAGUE BASEBALL TRYOUTS I would rank each player, on a scale of one to five, on their performance in the following categories: hitting, infield, outfield, speed, hustle, and attitude. Often, I would assign hustle and attitude more emphasis than any of the remaining skills. However, I also believed that attitude could always be changed. Therefore, I had no problem drafting a talented player with a bad attitude, particularly since most coaches would pass on such players during the first few rounds of the draft.

One of my first few draft picks in 2005 was Alvaro, a thin Hispanic kid who was trying out for the first time in this league. Fundamentally, he was a natural. I ranked him high in fielding and throwing the ball. His motions were smooth, he judged a fly ball well, and he consistently drove the ball into the outfield when hitting. However, no coaches knew who he was, and he walked around with attitude; when spoken to he barely responded, and rather than hustling in and out from his position, he chose a slow jog. Nevertheless, I drafted him as other coaches overlooked him. He would become one of my better players, would drastically change his attitude and become a player who showed up for every practice (early), and would again play for me on a future team.

Our practices during the season would incorporate traditional drills utilized by most high school or collegiate baseball programs; however, I would also occasionally integrate a "field trip" to the batting cages, the fielding and hitting game called pepper, a Wiffle ball game, a water balloon fight, a home run derby, and a baseball/trivia quiz show. At the end of every practice, I would split the players into two teams, assign a captain for each team, and one by one ask each team a series of five baseball and/or trivia questions, which they would discuss as a team before their captain gave their answer. Typical questions would be: "How many ways can a batter reach first base?" "Why is it called the bullpen?" "How did the Boston Red Sox get their name?" "Why is home plate a different size and shape than all the other bases?" "What do HR, RBI, and OBP stand for in baseball statistics?" At the beginning of every season, baseball trivia elicited groans and responses of "Oh hell no, Coach!" However, as the season progressed, they would actually remind me about baseball trivia at the end of every practice. "Coach, don't forget the trivia game . . . I'm just sayin' . . . I mean, I don't really care, but you always do it." The losing team in the trivia contest would have to run one lap around the entire field. They always ran.

After the first few practices of every season, each player received an official playbook. They were told to read it, learn it, and memorize it. It contained our game schedule, our field locations, our signs, our pickoff plays, our cutoff and relay scenarios, and tips on base running, bunting, hitting, and more. The book also had a special page where every player was given a nickname based on actions or observations from the first few practices. Nicknames in the Yankees season ranged from "Big Will" and "Aaron the Crab Killer" to "Bones" and "Grand Theft." Often, these nicknames stuck throughout the entire season.

We would lose the opening game of the 2005 season 31–4, which would also be defined as an ass whooping, a beating, a thrashing, or getting pulverized. According to Little League rules there is a ten-run rule: after five complete innings, or after the losing team bats in the fifth inning, the game is called if the winning team is leading by ten runs or more. We were losing 20–0 in the third inning. The opposing coach approached me after that inning and said, "OK, Coach, we can call this."

My response was, "Why? We still need to complete five innings."

"Come on, Coach," he insisted. "Your players are being humiliated. Let's put an end to this."

"No," I continued. "My players are playing baseball, which is what they signed up for . . . They may not be playing well, clearly, but we will keep playing until the umpire calls the game after five innings." He chuckled, mumbled, and walked away. The only words I could hear were something about the "new coach."

At the end of five innings, the umpire stopped the game.

After the game my players said, "Coach, why didn't you stop the game? We got the shit beat out of us, and those guys will never forget it!"

"Good," I responded. "However, I hope *we* never forget it, because we have to play them again. Plus, I assume you are here to play baseball, win or lose." We lost big, I told them, but we came back to score four runs and we played hard for as long as they would let us play. "*That* is the game of baseball!"

I was coaching other people's children—teaching them the game of baseball and to swing a bat like their lives depended on it. Little did I know how much being involved with that baseball team would help me later, when my life actually did depend on it—maybe not on swinging a bat, necessarily, but on maintaining that same sense of focus and determination to win—in my case, to survive—that I was trying to instill in them that first summer I coached. But that was later on. I first had to deal with the muscle spasms.

Chapter 5
The New Normal

MUSCLE SPASMS FROM A PINCHED NERVE? As the spasms increased, the people in my office took notice. After all, they were hanging on to my feet at times to help stop the spasms. I didn't want to waste time talking with them about my problem. My attitude, as always, was to work hard and focus on the business. My health was just a distraction.

But it distracted some of my staff to the point where they persuaded me to go back to my neurologist and confront him with my new symptoms. Admitting that I needed more help from the doctor was a big deal for me. At age forty-three, I had never had a regular physician, had never spent a night in a hospital, and probably hadn't missed a day of work because of illness in over ten years—not because I feared doctors, but merely because I preferred not to take the time. There's always something better to do, more important to do, more fun to do, than go see some doctor, right?

Nevertheless, in May 2005, I called my neurologist's office to schedule an appointment and was informed that mid to late July was the earliest they could get me in, as my fabulously fit doctor was going to be on vacation throughout June. I accepted an appointment for July 19.

The spasms were now occurring on a very regular basis. Therefore, waiting until the middle of July to finally find out what was going on did not sit well with me. My thoughts turned to Lyn's concerns about my driving (or the possibility that I shouldn't be) and Jessica's comments that this situation did not seem normal. I had yet to even inform my family back in Texas of the scenario, as I truly had no idea what the scenario was! How do you tell people what's wrong when you're not quite sure yourself?

Vacation for an entire month? A doctor? What happens to his patients? I never took vacation for an entire month! When I finally got in to see the doctor, the encounter was everything I had expected, and less.

"The situation has worsened," I told my doctor at that appointment. "The spasms are occurring about once a day, and my entire right leg and foot are increasingly experiencing total numbness."

"I've told you before," he said, looking through his black-rimmed glasses, "it's meralgia paresthetica. But if you'd like me to run more tests, I will."

Would I *like* him to? I actually felt that I was somehow bothering him—by not being the "good" patient who accepted his diagnosis. Still, I respected who he was, even though I felt that it should have been obvious that I would want to do further tests.

"Sure, I'd like to do more tests," I told him. "Wouldn't you?"

He shrugged. I couldn't understand his attitude. I thought that he would insist on doing more tests, if only to be on the safe side. "We'll take an MRI," he said in an offhanded way, "but I don't think there is a very high chance of finding anything. Your problems are caused by meralgia paresthetica. It's relatively common and non–life threatening."

I left the office actually hoping the MRI would reveal something—first, to give me some answers about my "condition," and second, to prove this guy wrong. The appointment for the MRI would be sometime in the coming weeks, I was told, and a follow-up appointment to review the results with my neurologist was prescheduled for August 29.

As I waited for the MRI, I went to a series of chiropractor visits, at the suggestion of my neurologist, who said the treatment might help "release" the pinched nerve. I wouldn't have gone out of my way to see a chiropractor, but I found a doctor in the same office building as my firm, so I figured I could take a walk downstairs twice a week for a while and check it out. After a few weeks of twice-a-week, hour-long sessions of getting my back and neck cracked, rolling around on large rubber balls like a two-year-old, and stretching and twisting in every way possible, I stopped the sessions. They weren't helping— well, the back massages were great, but the numbness in my leg was, if anything, getting worse.

After about two weeks of getting no phone calls back from the doctor's office pertaining to scheduling my MRI, I finally called the neurologist's office in late July to find out just what the hell was going on. How hard could it be—how long could it take—to schedule a simple exam? The only answer I got was that I would be called back soon with a status report. You do see the irony here, right? A status report on scheduling an appointment? At this point it wouldn't have surprised me if they had told me I needed an appointment to schedule an appointment.

By mid-August, I was feeling seriously frustrated by the continued lethargic attitude (not to mention the ineptitude) of my neurologist and his staff, and on August 12, 2005, I sent a letter to his office canceling the August 29 follow-up appointment we'd made one month earlier—the appointment that was supposed to allow us to review the results of the MRI . . . yes, that one, the one that never got scheduled. I also formally requested that all of my medical records with his office be sent directly to me.

I guess the thought of losing a billing account—um, I mean, losing a patient—at least got their attention because three days later, the office administrator called and left a message on my home phone, saying the MRI was never scheduled by the neurologist—the task had somehow "slipped through the cracks." Their lack of professionalism left me unmoved, and on August 20, I sent another letter, making my second request that all documentation relating to my visits to and treatment by their office—in short, everything in my medical file—be delivered to me.

I finally received all of the files from them in early

September and got busy making calls to several neurologists to schedule initial appointments. Effectively, I was starting over. From start to finish, the neurologist cost me ten months in trying to figure out what the heck was going on with my foot and leg.

Unfortunately, most of the new neurologists to whom I was reaching out to take over my case were telling me they were booked solid for weeks with patient appointments. They said that if I wanted to get in sooner, I would need to be referred by a general physician.

Again, I just didn't get it. The hoops the medical industry expects patients to jump through just to get through the door are amazing. Somehow, somebody has decided that patients—regular people who know their own bodies better than any doctor ever possibly could—are completely incapable of determining or deciding whether we need or want to see a specialist. Does this make any sense?

I knew that my leg was deteriorating. During the ten months I tried to work with the neurologist, the numbness and spasms became worse. I knew I had a problem, and I was finally admitting that I needed help. But I resented that fact, which made me even angrier with the medical establishment.

However, my anger fueled me to work harder—to work harder in my business, to work harder at coaching, and to work harder at enjoying my time with my family—all in spite of whatever was going on with my leg. However, I also worked harder at trying to find that one rebel doctor, that one specialist, who would see me without a referral from a general physician.

I was busy as usual and mostly just ignored what was going on with my leg, confident the MRI would answer a lot of questions. Life went on, more or less, as normal: It was plenty hectic, brimming with lots to do, with a lot of deadlines to keep the pressure on—just the way I like it. Of course, Lyn and the kids were at the top of my priority list.

Chapter 6

The Proposal

LYN WAS SOMEONE I WAS SUPPOSED TO MEET. Our souls appeared drawn together. I first met Lyn at a wedding in Tucson. Lauri, my first wife, and I were attending the wedding of a couple of friends. Lyn was also attending the wedding. At the reception I asked the groom, "Who's the bridesmaid in the yellow dress?" To this day Lyn asserts that she wasn't wearing a yellow dress; however, my visualization of her reveals a yellow dress, so yellow dress it is! At that time Lyn was single and I was married.

Our next meeting would be at a birthday party. The daughter of the same couple, Rylee, was celebrating her third birthday. Briana and I were invited—I was then divorced. Lyn, her husband—Lyn was then married—and Adam and Olivia were also invited. Lyn attended the party with Adam and Olivia, but the husband was a no-show. That worked for me! The party was at a local amusement park, and at one point during the day, Lyn, Adam, Olivia, Briana, and I all ended up on the same ride, in the same car. It was one of those whirlybird rides where the bar smashes into your crotch and you spin around and around. As I spun, I remember thinking, "Wow, Lyn is absolutely stunning!" She had a big smile, big brown eyes, and a petite body.

We would meet for the next two years, annually, at Rylee's fourth and fifth birthday parties. While I remained single, Lyn remained married. We would always talk and catch up while the kids played and partied. Ultimately, we would run into each other at a few happy hours, again with mutual friends, and I would hear that she and her husband had separated. I eventually extended an offer to go see a movie sometime, get a drink, or hang out with the kids. The prospect never materialized until a Saturday afternoon when I received a call at my office (yes, I was working on a Saturday). Lyn indicated that she had two tickets to *Les Misérables*, for that same day, and her date (a female friend, or so she claims) had turned up sick. I had about three hours to wrap up my work, drive home, take a shower, change clothes, and drive over and pick her up so we could grab some dinner before the show. No problem. That would be known as our first date. Clearly, and regardless of how she tells the story, she pursued me!

We dated for two years and then got engaged. I proposed to Lyn on her birthday—her fortieth birthday. For her, it was a typical birthday celebration: one that incorporated all five of us. The five that would soon become one family. To remind her she was turning forty, as a thoughtful boyfriend should, I bought her forty gifts. Every tenth gift would lead her to a "destination." After she opened the first nine gifts, the tenth was lunch at Carolina's, her favorite Mexican restaurant. So, we departed from the house where she lived with Adam and Olivia and headed over to Carolina's, where we enjoyed lunch and Lyn opened the next ten gifts.

Of course, the three kids were documenting every step of the event via a video recorder. And we all know how the video turns out when eight-, nine-, and ten-year-old kids are video-taping—feet are videotaped, close-up shots are way too close, and people we don't even know show up in the video. Nevertheless, their documentation of the event added an interesting twist.

The twentieth gift guided us over to my and Briana's house, where the next ten gifts were waiting. Now at this point, Lyn fully believed this was only a birthday celebration, as did Adam and Olivia. Briana was completely aware of the plan, as two weeks earlier Briana and I had spent a weekend away, at a local resort, where I told her I wanted to propose to Lyn. I told Briana I needed her blessing. Without hesitation she exploded with excitement, and the two of us had a great weekend as well as sharing a secret. When Lyn opened her thirtieth gift, which was a sketch of the Hermosa Inn, she knew the meaning behind the next destination. Lon's restaurant at the Hermosa Inn, in Paradise Valley, Arizona, was where I took Lyn on our third date and where we experienced our first kiss. The framed drawing was a charcoal sketch by none other than me. As a child I loved to draw, so although I was a little rusty, I tried my hand at this sketch. She recognized the inn from the sketch, so I suppose it wasn't too horrible. Off we went.

As we arrived at the inn, I bought Lyn a drink and told her

to have a seat at the bar. "I need to take a walk with Briana, Adam, and Olivia," I stated. "You can wait here while we prepare the final ten gifts."

"No problem," she calmly replied, with no idea whatsoever what was about to happen. On this walk Briana and I told Adam and Olivia the plan. They listened intently until I posed the question to both of them: "I need to know from both of you if it's OK if I ask your mom to marry me." Olivia smiled and said, "Yes, yes, yes!" Adam paused, then asked, "You mean you're going to be our stepdad?"

"That's right," I replied. "Are you OK with this?"

"Yes, I think I would like that," Adam firmly replied.

When we returned to Lyn, she continued to open her gifts. Some were significant, others were not. ChapStick, lotion, and a candle would periodically appear as my creativity began to wane after so many gifts. But the thirty-seventh gift was the following poem I wrote. As I read the poem to her, we were standing in the exact spot where we first kissed.

In my 37th year my life would change when I met someone whom I had known.

Though from afar our paths did cross, we'd soon discover how our lives would grow.

I came to love her laugh, her smile, her sneeze.

I came to love when she was cold with the very slightest breeze.

She became my running partner, my driving mate, and my friend.

She became the person whose faith in me would never end.

She showed me "rubs," I showed her "busts."

We saw beaches and river walks, and touring a swamp became a must.

We fell from the sky and rode coasters to heaven.

We spent hours in a van with the two of us, plus seven.

But of all the memories . . . there is one I remember most;

For it was in this very spot, where we first kissed.

So in this spot I prepare a toast.

To all the times we've shared together . . .

To all the times we've yet to see . . .

I love you Lyn with all my heart . . .

And with this 37th gift . . . ask for you to marry me!

Throughout the poem, she laughed with each line, reminiscing with each memory. However, when I read the final line, she stood speechless with her mouth wide open. Tears began to stream from her eyes. She looked at Briana, at Adam, at Olivia. They were smiling and giggling. "We know, Mom!" After the initial shock, and after realizing that everyone knew about this, and, more important, that everyone was OK with this, she finally said "yes."

In the weeks prior to my marriage to Lyn, Briana, then eleven years old, practiced and perfected a duet performance with me of the Nat King Cole and Natalie Cole version of "Unforgettable." During the wedding reception, we completely surprised Lyn (again) when I went to the front of the banquet room, took the microphone from the band, and announced to Lyn and everyone at the reception that the song for our first dance would be a recording of "Unforgettable"—performed not by the famous father-daughter Cole duo, but by Lyn's new, not-so-famous husband and daughter.

Chapter 7

Antiques

THE PRIMARY FOCUS, FOR BOTH LYN AND ME, was our kids. As a family we would travel together, go to the zoo, go to amusement parks, go swimming, have parties, and do anything and everything kid related. However, during our non-kid time, Lyn and I would jog together, go on (work-related) inspections together, shop together, work out together, and talk, talk, and talk. Lyn has told me I'm never at a loss for words. Eventually, more and more of the time, we found ourselves talking about opening an antiques store.

Why an antiques store? As a kid, I grew up miserably shuffling through antiques malls, flea markets, auctions, and other such places as my parents took to antiquing as a hobby and gave my sister and me no other choice than to participate in this activity. Consequently, I decided to take some sort of an interest, so I began collecting busts at about the age of ten. My first two were President Washington and President Lincoln. Through the years, I managed to collect hundreds of busts; however, I ultimately sold about two hundred small, insignificant "heads," and I currently maintain only a bust collection of U.S. presidents. The current challenge is locating busts of obscure presidents to complete my collection.

Lyn and I had also shared an interest in antiques as a hobby—we often scoured antiques stores for "retro" items to decorate our home, and we even began periodically selling extra finds in antiques mall booths. As we traipsed through store after store over the years, we found most antiques shops to be essentially boring, disorganized, and cluttered. Of course, my entrepreneurial instincts kicked in, and we both thought the same thing: "Let's do it right." Which meant doing it differently.

We found a space, and as we worked on it, Lyn and I spent quite a bit of time down there—we dedicated days and nights to stripping the floors, building walls, and painting. At the same time, I was also collaborating with the director of operations for my appraisal company, Allan Thorson, on creating space for a recording studio in the back of the building. Allan, whom I call Al, is a musician when he's not helping me run my business, and he had always piddled around in the recording business. I had a minority interest in his fledgling studio but also was putting up the real estate to help him pursue his dream.

My motives weren't completely altruistic, however. My daughter, Briana, had spent her entire childhood performing in plays, pageants, and talent and dance competitions. From about the age of two, Briana would talk me into performing scenes from a play or movie nearly every night. She'd use a plastic baseball bat as a fake microphone to belt out her favorite songs from all the Disney movies. Yes, I admit it—I'd bought the bat for a two-year-old girl, hoping she'd have a little tomboy in her. It didn't work, but she did become a major baseball fan.

My little girl was a singer and performer from the start. So jump-starting Al's recording business was also a way for me to help my daughter pursue her dreams. Years later, Briana mixed her interest in baseball and music when she was selected not just once, but twice, to perform the national anthem at an Arizona Diamondbacks professional baseball game. After one of the anthems, Randy Johnson called out her name as we walked off the field and said, "Nice job!"

At the beginning of August, Al's studio was operational, and we celebrated the grand opening of our antiques store, BOA Antiques and Attitudes (BOA comprised the first initial of each our children: Briana, Olivia, and Adam). We'd been fortunate to get some television publicity for the event, and we sold a few thousand dollars' worth of inventory right out of the gate. Lyn had retired from her banking career earlier in the year and was ready to operate and manage the store. Instead of the usual one-room jumble, we divided our store into six distinct shopping experiences. As customers moved through the store, they essentially were journeying through "time capsules"—from the 1920s and 1930s, with deco mirrors and antique rockers, to a diner that showcased items from the 1940s and 1950s, to a 1960s- and 1970s-themed area with peace signs and even a 1972 AMC Gremlin automobile, which sat in the middle of the room and was for sale for a mere $1,500. It sold quickly.

Finally, customers finished their journey in a themed children's room, with vintage furniture and kids' items, including Hula-Hoops, Frisbees, and vintage lunch boxes.

1960s/70s Room in BOA Antiques & Attitudes

Believe it or not, even after we opened the store, I guess I didn't think I had my hand in enough pots. That same summer, despite the alternating twitching and lifeless numbness of my right leg, running my appraisal business, opening a new retail business, and being involved with the start-up of the recording studio, I was developing another business—an online showcase of commercial real estate available for sale and lease that provided virtual tours of the properties. Instead of spending days touring building after building and suite after suite, prospective lessees or buyers could preview properties online in one-tenth the time it would take to drive around to all the properties and walk through them in person.

In addition, I was coaching Little League baseball. The Yankees had finished my first season one game above .500—nothing to write home about, but a respectful season. I had been accepted as a coach, was initiated into the league, and had earned my stripes. As with any community service organization, politics were abundant. I was set for season two.

I like to have a lot of irons in the fire, but by late summer 2005, even I recognized that I was stretched a bit thin. I recognized it, but it didn't feel like a bad thing. People have always either applauded or criticized me for doing too much. But for me, there's no such thing as too much. I've always had many diverse interests and have felt an inner push to pursue them—to see what I could do, to take an idea and play it out. The point wasn't so much whether I succeeded or failed as it was simply to try something out. I was happiest when I had a lot of things cooking, and if it meant I slept fewer hours each night, worked longer into the night, or had to swing a paintbrush on Sunday afternoon, that was fine with me. I was growing my business, helping a loyal employee pursue his own dreams, getting the antiques business off the ground with my wife, and raising our three children—Briana was in high school, Adam was in eighth grade, and Olivia was in seventh grade. I had a medical condition, but I didn't know whether it was affecting my performance—in business, as a coach, or with my family. In fact, I didn't even know I had a medical condition.

For the moment, life was good.

Chapter 8

It's Not Brain Surgery

(OH, WAIT A MINUTE . . . YES IT IS)

LIFE WAS GOOD . . . right up until it wasn't.

Ultimately, I succeeded in finding a doctor to replace the neurologist who diagnosed a pinched nerve. She agreed to see me within a matter of days, and on September 20 I met with Dr. Bronislava Shafran, a small, older, dark-skinned woman who had an accent and spoke very loudly—she pretty much yelled most of the time. But the rest of her demeanor was so professional, the shouting seemed harmless. Her office was modest and simple—no fancy furniture or artwork—but I felt I'd finally found someone who was focused, logical, and taking my situation seriously.

Dr. Shafran administered an office exam and reviewed my records from the previous neurologist as I sat in her office.

After about fifteen minutes, she looked up from the records and said, "I think your muscle spasms are actually seizures. Brain seizures, in fact."

"Your first neurologist obviously didn't know what he was talking about," she shouted.

Dr. Shafran didn't pull any punches, and I admired that. At first I felt relieved and vindicated. Finally, finally someone was getting to the truth of my condition. Then, after I processed the information for a few seconds, reality began to sink in. Brain seizures were serious business, a lot more serious than a pinched nerve. So, what then?

Honestly, hearing that I had brain seizures did nothing to change my attitude about my condition, or my life. A bad cold or the flu. A pinched nerve or brain seizures. I wasn't about to have any medical condition interfere with my work, or my life.

The icing on the cake of my visit—if there can be icing on a doctor's visit where you learn you're having brain seizures— was that before I left her office, Dr. Shafran had her assistant immediately schedule an MRI for September 23, to be followed by an electroencephalogram (EEG) on September 27. Thank God for Dr. Shafran!

I assume that most people would have asked themselves, "Why am I having brain seizures?" "Should I tell my family?" I really didn't have any of these thoughts. Rather, I went home, met with my family—including all three kids, who were then twelve, thirteen, and fourteen years old—and told them I had been having brain seizures all this time.

Briana asked, "Dad, what's causing the brain seizures?"

I responded, "We will soon find out, finally!"

A day after my EEG, September 28, I was sitting at my

desk, with, as usual, several appraisal reports piled in front of me—some I was writing, others I was reviewing—when Dr. Shafran called my office. Although I didn't want to be interrupted, I took the call.

"I have reviewed the results of your exams, the MRI and EEG," she announced in her loud voice. "You have a tumor growing inside your brain. About the size of a plum. You need to come to my office tomorrow. Any time will work, just be there."

As I hung up the phone, I asked myself, "Is a doctor really supposed to tell me this kind of thing over the phone?"

That was Dr. Shafran. I appreciated her blunt style. It was like my own style: no BS and straight to the point.

Still, my interpretation of the phone call was, "You are going to die! Hurry up and get your ass in my office! You don't have much time!"

I'd never really worried too much about dying, and even hearing that I had a tumor in my brain didn't change my attitude. I thought that maybe I should leave the office and drive around in my car, gathering my thoughts. After all, this is what people did in all the movies. But I wasn't really sure where I should drive. I knew I would just aimlessly point my car in one direction and then another, and it all seemed to be a colossal waste of gas and time. So I figured I might as well stay at my office, maybe get some work done. I didn't feel the need to get emotional about the problem. I knew it was there. I wanted to ignore it and get on with my life. I did understand that I had to call my wife and tell her the news. As I dialed her number, I didn't know what I was going to say.

"Hello, Lyn?"

"Yes."

"I just talked with the doctor, and I have a tumor growing in my brain."

There was silence on the other end of the line. Then Lyn asked, "What does that mean?"

"I'm not quite sure how long I have to live."

The phone was silent. We ended the conversation by indicating that we would talk more that night, a night when all three of our kids were with their other parents. When I arrived home, I spent up to an hour explaining, as accurately as possible, my conversation with Dr. Shafran. Lyn listened.

"Do you know anyone who's had a brain tumor?" she asked.

"No, do you?"

"No."

"I'm really not sure," I continued, "whether people live with brain tumors, or die from them. But I'll ask Dr. Shafran tomorrow."

"Do you want me to go with you?" Lyn asked.

"No, you have the store, and it will be tough to get someone to fill in on short notice. I'll go by myself."

If, in fact, death was a possibility, I wanted to hear it by myself and process it by myself. Plus, I knew it would be extremely emotional for Lyn to hear. As a result, I wanted to tell Lyn myself, if necessary. I spent the remainder of the night on the phone with my family in Texas: my mom, my dad, and my sister. For each of them the news was especially startling, as all three had received little information from me up to this point. I wasn't particularly worried about my condition because

I chose not to be. I had other things to worry about, like work, baseball, and BOA Antiques and Attitudes.

The next morning, I met with Dr. Shafran. Although she probably was explaining a lot of important things to me, I could concentrate only on the one question I wanted to ask. Finally, I blurted it out.

"How long do I have to live?"

"Did I say you were going to die?" she yelled back at me. "What makes you think you're going to die? Nobody said you were going to die!"

That was all I needed to hear. If the doctor thought I wasn't going to die, that was good enough for me. I had spent enough time thinking about the ultimate consequences. I didn't like thinking about it. It felt self-indulgent to me, or maybe it was easier for me to bury myself in activities and avoid facing reality. Given the good news, I remained glad I had decided to see Dr. Shafran by myself.

However, I knew that Lyn was anxiously awaiting my phone call. Instead of calling her, I drove straight to the store, pulled into the parking lot, and walked in the front door. She was with a customer, so I just strolled around the store as if I were a customer who was stopping by for the first time. Although Lyn was attentive to her customer, her eyes continually glanced in my direction, attempting to read my face or my body language, or get some sort of indication as to the news I had received. Once the customer finished the purchase and left the store, Lyn made a beeline in my direction.

"Well?"

"Well," I calmly stated, "I think our '60s/'70s room is our best section."

No response. However, her eyes started to water and she wrapped her arms around me. She knew me. She knew the answer.

Within days, Dr. Shafran had scheduled a consultation with Dr. Peter Nakaji, a neurosurgeon at Barrows Neurological Institute, at St. Joseph's Hospital and Medical Center in Phoenix; the institute was internationally recognized as a leader in neurological research and patient care.

My first consultation with Dr. Nakaji was on October 18. Of Asian descent and appearing to be in his late thirties, Dr. Nakaji was confident, assuring, and calm; I immediately felt comfortable with him and felt I was with the right doctor.

Dr. Nakaji described my tumor to me. It was a hemangiopericytoma, a type of very rare tumor involving blood vessels and soft tissues; he told me it was benign.

I liked the fact that I had a "very rare" tumor almost as much as I liked hearing that it was benign. But I didn't like either aspect well enough to keep it; I wanted the feeling back in my legs, and I didn't want to take any chances.

"Hemangiopericytomas often are painless masses which can originate anywhere in the body where there are capillaries," Dr. Nakaji explained. "They can be either benign or malignant and can metastasize, or spread, to other areas in the body, primarily the lungs and bones. The preferred surgical treatment is the endoscopic endonasal approach to remove the tumor—an innovative, minimally invasive technique that uses the nose and nasal cavities as natural corridors to access hard-to-reach tumors."

The new technique might be "minimally invasive," but all I could think was, "No, thank you very much. I think I would just prefer to have my skull cracked open, please, for the tumor removal, because the endonasal approach brought to mind a scene from the movie *Total Recall* where Arnold Schwarzenegger jams a self-guiding bug-removal mechanism way up into his nose until he hears a "crunch."

Turned out I didn't have to worry about "pulling an Arnold," fortunately (or unfortunately?). Because of the large size of my tumor, the endoscopic approach would not be an option after all.

We scheduled an appointment for three weeks later, on November 7, for Dr. Nakaji to perform a seven-hour surgery to open my skull and remove the tumor from my brain.

Lucky me. It really was going to be brain surgery.

Chapter 9

Letting Go

NOW THAT I KNEW I HAD A BRAIN TUMOR, I didn't really feel any different than when I didn't know it existed. I did think, "Wow, I ran that last marathon with that plum of a tumor . . . no wonder my time sucked so bad!"

When I explained the tumor to the kids, they were calm, most likely because I was calm. I told them I had the best surgeon, that I was hoping to get the feeling back in my leg, and that everything was going to be fine. We didn't cry, we didn't talk about whether I was going to die, we didn't hang our heads. None of us knew what we were facing, but as always we were optimistic. Until the surgery, life just went on.

I did feel anger at the first neurologist I visited. A lot of people suggested that I pursue some form of litigation against him because of his failure to diagnose coupled with his arrogance and general incompetence.

I did speak once to an attorney who specialized in malpractice cases. He was the brother of an employee of mine, and I knew he'd give it to me straight. His opinion was that it would be difficult to prove just how much the tumor had grown or accurately predict what further complications I might suffer from as a result of the nearly yearlong delay during which the first neurologist failed to diagnose the tumor. Ultimately, he felt that a settlement, if achievable, would be in the ballpark of $250,000.

I considered taking legal action, but I decided instead that I could use my energy much better by focusing on beating the tumor, getting healthy, and moving on with my life. That neurologist was probably still keeping super-fit by hiking or cycling through Scottsdale. I certainly hope he's not practicing medicine. As for me, I was focusing on work.

Similar to how I discussed the upcoming surgery with my family, I called a meeting with all of the employees in my company and informed them of the scenario. The room was quiet, but I assured them that this was a minor setback. No one needed to worry about his job, no one needed to be concerned with her workload, and certainly no one needed to worry about me. I wasn't sure how long I would be gone from the company, but I guaranteed them I would be in daily contact with three people, Allan, Jessica, and Tom, all of whom had worked at the company for years and years. It would be business as usual at Lefevers Viewpoint Group. Over 75 regular company clients were notified via the following e-mail:

> I hope this e-mail finds all well. I first want to thank
> all clients of Lefevers Viewpoint Group, Inc. for
> your business and for your loyalty. I was recently

diagnosed with a brain tumor and am scheduled
for surgery on November 7. It is not life-threatening,
and I plan to return to my company as soon as
possible after the surgery. In the meantime I have
an incredible staff of appraisers and administrators
who will serve your every need. As always, appraisal
assignments will be bid on, and quality appraisal
reports will be completed and delivered in a timely
manner. Any appraisal matters can be directed to
Tom Raynak, MAI, who has been with the company
for ten years, and all administrative topics will be
resolved by Allan Thorson, an employee of five
years. Thank you, and I will talk to all very soon.

I never considered the surgery to be life-threatening, and
I fully believed (key word "believed") that the numbness in
my leg would disappear. I downplayed my situation, as I felt
strongly that I was protecting myself, my family, my company,
and my employees. My employees had to believe I would be
back to work, and the clients of the company needed to feel
confident that they could continue doing business with Lefevers Viewpoint Group. Yet, despite my confidence, my calmness, and my assurance to my employees, one of my appraisers
resigned. He had been with the company for three years, we
got along well, and he was a good appraiser. Nevertheless, his
aunt had recently died from a brain tumor, and he was convinced I would never return to the company. His departure
shocked some employees and concerned others.

Finally, the day for my surgery arrived.

Chapter 10

Don't Put the Gown on Without Asking Questions

CHECK-IN AT THE HOSPITAL WAS 8:00 A.M., November 7, 2005, with surgery scheduled for 2:00 p.m. I wasn't quite sure what I would be doing for six long hours, but the hospital staff assured me that I would need ample time for "signing of documents, waivers, etc.," and that I would spend a lot of time "pretesting." Plus, if everything went well, they said they could take me into surgery early. Therefore, around 8:30 a.m., I stripped off my clothes, put the hospital gown on, and followed every instruction I was given. I checked the box to donate my tumor to scientific study, but the businessman in me still managed to ask if I was going to get a tax credit for my donation. ("No," was their polite, if astonished, answer. What? Hadn't anyone asked that question before?)

I was finished with the documentation, pre-testing, and all the rest within a few hours, and I was instructed to stay in my room, or at least stay close by. The prospect of spending several hours in my room was not appealing, especially since my entire family was passing time roaming the hospital. I decided to take off the gown, put my clothes back on, and mosey around with them. I walked up to the nearest nurse and said, "I'll be down in the cafeteria and will check back every half hour or so."

The nurse gave me a long, astonished look and slowly stated, "No, you really need to keep the gown on, stay close by, and be prepared at any moment for surgery."

"But my surgery isn't scheduled for hours."

"Yes, but they could call you in early," she continued.

"OK, here's my cell phone number," I suggested. "Call me if surgery is earlier than scheduled and I will be here in no time."

"All right," she gave in, "but could you at least put the gown back on so you won't have to take the time to change?"

"I'll have my cell phone with me at all times, will check back with you every thirty minutes, and won't eat or drink anything; however, I will not put that gown on and walk around the hospital with my bare, glowing white ass hanging out."

Finally she gave me another one of her long stares and nodded. I assumed this was a sign of assent, so off I went to the cafeteria, where I was able to spend the next few hours with Lyn and Briana, Adam, Olivia, as well as my dad, mom, and sister, who had all flown in from Texas to be there for the surgery.

For the most part the conversation comprised catching up with my family. My parents and my sister asked our kids a lot of questions about their schooling, their sporting events, their dance performances, and such. Little of the conversation had much to do with me or the surgery.

On one of my check-ins, the nurses told me that it was nearing time to go into surgery. I put my hospital gown back on and lay down on the gurney. I was wheeled into a waiting room, where other patients lay on gurneys. We were separated only by thin curtains, and each patient was allowed visits by two family members at a time. Two by two my family members stood by my side; we casually visited to pass the time.

Finally, my number was called, and the staff began to drip a drug into my arm. My last two visitors were Lyn and Briana. For nearly the first time, Briana was upset. She teared up and could only muster three words: "I love you." I'm sure the sight of her father lying on a gurney, about to be rolled into a surgery room to have his head cracked open, finally took its toll. I fought to hold back my tears, but to no avail. Tears streamed down my face from the thought of the fear my daughter was likely experiencing. The drip was taking effect, and as the lights got dimmer and dimmer, my last words to Briana were, "I love you too . . . see you soon!"

Hours later, as I stretched out on a gurney being wheeled down a hospital corridor, I opened my eyes.

"What time is it?" I asked. "How long was the surgery? Did they get the entire tumor?" And maybe most important, "When do I get a sponge bath?"

My gurney ride ended in a private room in the intensive care unit (ICU), where I was to spend the night. The surgery commenced at 2:00 p.m. and took seven hours, so it was already 9:00 p.m., and visitors were no longer allowed in the ICU. Lyn, however, persuaded the nurses to allow visitors two at a time . . . she knows me well and was very confident I wouldn't have it any other way. She and Briana were the first two visitors, and as I saw Briana, my very first comment was, "Hey, your hair wasn't braided when I went into surgery."

Briana laughed and said, "Dad, it was seven hours . . . a lot of things happened while you were in surgery."

We talked for about ten minutes. I asked what they did for seven hours, who stayed at the hospital, and what my head looked like. "Everyone stayed and waited," they said. "We mostly talked, read books, and took walks around the hospital." And: "Your head is partially shaved, the scar is about five inches, and you have about twenty staples in your skull."

Well, that about sums it up, I thought. As they left, I managed to flash my bare ass to them. Not quite sure why I felt compelled to do that, other than that as a forty-three-year-old, it was the first time in my life I would spend the night in a hospital, and the whole gown thing (with nothing underneath) was new to me.

Although I was very content the surgery was over, and although the painkilling drug was effectively working its way through my system, I can't say that I had a restful sleep my first night in the ICU. I did, however, learn the term "code blue," as every time this term was blasted over the speaker system, I could hear pattering feet outside my door. Further, my next-door neighbor found it necessary to yell and cuss at every person who walked by wearing a white coat. "Hey, asshole, I need some drugs in here . . . Help me—somebody help me! . . . Hey, I can't stand the pain—get me some fucking drugs!" If I could have gotten myself out of bed, I think I would have introduced his face to my pillow.

Through the night, the nurse and I had numerous conversations about "code blue," my neighbor, and other subjects. I learned that "code blue" meant someone had stopped breathing (unfortunately *not* my neighbor), and I learned that my neighbor was perfectly fine and adequately medicated in spite of his spewing accusations. However, the nurse never would tell me why he was in the ICU—hospital rules.

The morning couldn't have come soon enough, so I wasn't the slightest bit upset when she came back in and woke me up early for more tests. She definitely appreciated my attitude, and therefore I managed to persuade her to smuggle a telephone into my room so I could wake up my family. ICU patients didn't have telephones in their rooms for obvious reasons, as exemplified by my neighbor's actions.

The nurse stood next to me as I called Lyn on my temporary phone.

"Hello?" Lyn said.

I could tell by the sound of her voice that I had woken her up.

"Hello, this is Dr. Nakaji," I said, imitating the doctor's voice as well as I could.

"Good morning, doctor," she said, sounding apprehensive.

"Mrs. Lefevers, Jay did not make it through the night."

Silence. *Oh no*, I thought. *Maybe I've gone too far.*

Silence. "Lyn, Lyn, it's me, Jay. I was just joking. I'm fine."

A moment more of silence, then Lyn scolded, "What are you doing . . . you can't do that! I'm so glad you're OK! You must be OK, 'cause you still have your sense of humor!"

I found it humorous; Lyn considered it typical for me;

and others—when they heard about it—said it was downright cruel. The nurse witnessed the conversation and took the phone away from me, saying, "No more calls for you!"

Later that day I was moved to a private room, where I subsequently had visits from my neurosurgeon, therapists, nurses, and other hospital staff. I later asked to see the tumor that had been causing me so much trouble, but Dr. Nakaji said it was a "bloody mess" and not something I wanted to see.

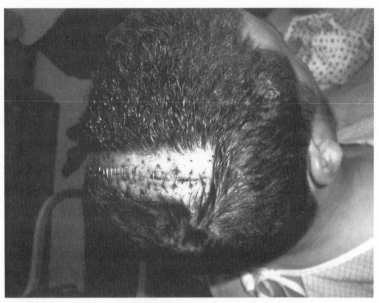

20+ staples . . . and a bad haircut!

The MRIs I had after surgery would reveal that the operation had been extremely successful, with complete removal of the tumor. However, my leg still felt numb. My doctor told me that the tumor removal process had required partial scraping of surrounding brain tissue, which—unfortunately—resulted in increased nerve damage and worsening of the lack of sensitivity or feeling in my leg. As Dr. Nakaji explained, "We had hoped [that], like a grape, it would have had a skin on it, so we could have essentially peeled the tumor off your brain." But my case wasn't so simple. My tumor wasn't as easy as a grape being peeled, and essentially, he told me, the numbness was severely enhanced in my right leg—which most likely would not change for the rest of my life.

Chapter 11

Dealing with It

A BUNCH OF QUESTIONS SWAM IN MY HEAD. After all, I'd been nearly 100 percent convinced that the feeling in my leg would completely return after the surgery. I wasn't really prepared for it not to come back fully, and so I had absolutely no idea what to expect.

What did this mean? Would I walk funny? Would I ever run again? Was it to feel as though I had an artificial leg? And how do people walk with artificial legs anyway? How do they control movement of something attached to their body that they can't feel? Would my leg change color? Would it suffer from atrophy and ultimately leave me with one regular-size leg and one puny, skinny leg? For now, I was still hopeful the feeling might eventually come back. If it didn't, I figured I would cross other bridges when I got to them.

The first night in the private room, one guest was allowed to stay. Briana and I had a sleepover. The nurses would wake me up periodically throughout the night for tests, and Briana would always wake up and see if I needed any help, or any cranberry juice.

"Why did they want me to drink cranberry juice?" I wondered.

I later found out that cranberry juice is low in calories, an excellent source of vitamin C, a very good source of dietary fiber, and a good source of manganese and vitamin K. Cranberries contain zero cholesterol, and the total fat composition is only 0.1 grams, which makes it a very low-fat, healthy drink. Some things about the health system actually did make sense.

The surgery had been on Monday night. By the time Wednesday rolled around, I was getting a little bored. The therapists made their regular visits, walking me through the hallways and up and down the stairs, but for the most part I spent the day sitting in bed with Lyn, Briana, Adam, and Olivia hanging around my bedside to keep me company.

During this time, my family discovered the television show *Deal or No Deal*. I got so bored watching the show that I began to act like a guy who didn't choose the right briefcase and then lost it on camera. "Howie, this sucks," I said in my bed, my head completely bandaged. "I didn't win anything. This show is fixed!" We all had a good laugh over that, Frankenstein chewing out Howie Mandel.

I'd been told that if everything went well, I should be able to go home over the weekend, or five to six days after surgery. I needed to get out of the hospital, but the rules were clear and enforced. In order to leave, I needed to prove I could keep my food down; I had to be able to walk on my own; and I absolutely could not leave until I had at least one successful bowel movement. Really? I had to prove I was capable of dropping the kids off at the pool just to get a pass to go home? It was another instance that made my medical experience more humorous than horrifying.

I was already eating, keeping my food down, and walking around by Tuesday afternoon, one day after surgery; one simple bowel movement and I figured I'd be on my way home no later than Wednesday afternoon or evening. My doctor had made it clear that it was atypical for a patient to be released two days after a seven-hour brain surgery. However, by Wednesday morning, with all the progress I was making in other areas, my neurosurgeon had checked me over and given the green light for my release that evening—pending the much-anticipated bowel movement, which was, unfortunately, not happening fast enough for me.

Somewhere between 4:00 and 5:00 p.m., two days after my surgery, I received my release. The nurse showed up at my room with a wheelchair, which I declined—not to impress anyone nor to prove a point, but simply because I wanted to walk. I wanted to prove to myself that I once again had control of my body and my life. I knew that I would be responsible for my own recovery, not a nurse or a therapist. As for the bowel movement . . . it never happened. I lied.

Chapter 12

Back to Work

THAT WEDNESDAY NIGHT—NOVEMBER 9, 2005— I came home from the hospital. My sister and my mom flew back to Texas early the next morning, and on Friday, Lyn, my dad, and I went antiques shopping. Makes sense, right? After all, if I were to stay at home, lying around all day in bed, I might as well return to the hospital, put the gown back on, and watch *Deal or No Deal*. I wasn't about to waste my first day back in the land of the living, and searching for bargain items to resell in our antiques store seemed like a good way to ease back into my so-called "regular" life.

The only concession I made to my condition was to throw on a baseball cap. The doctors, instead of stitching me up like in the old days, had used heavy-duty staples, which look like the type you might see shooting out of your neighbor's Stanley staple gun while he puts shingles on a roof. Well, at least I knew there was small chance of my scalp coming apart at the seams. That wouldn't be pretty.

At home, my family was already accustomed to seeing the five inches of staples—altogether about 20 of them—that were holding my postsurgery scalp together. I wasn't that self-conscious about showing my head in public. But I didn't want to scare any old ladies. Hence the baseball cap.

Shopping for antiques was a great diversion. I didn't have any headaches or bad reaction to the surgery. My leg was still numb and turning out to be somewhat worse than it had been before. But, I felt like I was in control, enjoying Lyn and my dad's company as if the surgery had never happened.

The rest of the first weekend at home passed fairly quietly. No big talks, though we did chat about the whole hospital experience as a family. But there were no big "Were you afraid you were going to die?" kinds of things. Just a normal (well, relatively speaking) family weekend.

After a few hours of antiques shopping, during which time Lyn and my dad regularly asked if I was OK, we headed home. There, I sat in bed most of the time, propped up (as instructed . . . these instructions I followed), drank cranberry juice, and watched TV. The cranberry juice was familiar, and I was home. I was at peace.

After a weekend of rest and relaxation, I was anxious to get back to work. It had been a full week out of the office, and though I knew that my appraisal company was in good hands with my staff and management team, I wanted to get back to work. Lyn wasn't sure I should be going back to work just seven days out from surgery, but because I was insistent, she called my neurosurgeon to get his opinion. If he was cool with it, she would be too, she said.

"It may be atypical," Dr. Nakaji said when Lyn asked him if it was normal for someone who'd had a tumor removed from his brain to go back to work just a week later. "But let him go back to work," he advised. "His body will let him know when it has had enough."

So, that Monday, exactly seven days after my surgery, I walked through the doors of Lefevers Viewpoint Group . . . with my baseball cap on, of course . . . and got back to work. It was great to be back. I felt very fortunate: fortunate to be back so quickly, and fortunate to have a great company with hard-working people by my side. My plan was to work at least half days, but the days went by so quickly that I ended up working full days. Most employees were hesitant to tax me with any appraisal questions or assignment complications; it was a nice change and certainly made the day more relaxed. I felt a little ridiculous and unprofessional with my baseball cap, which I was constantly taking off throughout the day to show off my scar and my staples. I think this act made them stay away more, although that wasn't my intention.

Subsequent to the surgery, my walk was exaggerated—I lifted my right leg too high and still often tripped over my right foot, which would drag along the ground. The hospital highly recommended I visit a therapist at least once a week to relearn how to walk with what was shaping up to be a lifelong condition of having a numb leg and foot. They felt I needed to train my brain to operate a leg that it—the brain—didn't acknowledge, and they warned that if I continued to walk in the exaggerated, semi-dragging way I was, there was serious potential that I would throw my hips out of alignment.

However, at this point, after almost two years of being in and out of doctors' offices, I wasn't interested in any more doctor visits than necessary. I figured that if I was able to learn to walk at age one, I could certainly relearn to walk at age forty-three. I didn't see how anyone else could help me learn to walk. It was my body, and I had to control it. Therefore, my daily therapy session was with myself—walking, walking, and more walking.

It wasn't easy. At first, I had to will my leg to move. I had problems going up stairs. I struggled to run, and I certainly labored with any sport, such as racquetball. My ankle would easily twist, and my toes would often irregularly rub against my shoes; although I was unable to feel the latter, I would discover the result when I got home after work, took off my shoes, and found blistered, bloodied, or scraped toes. My right foot was constantly getting tangled under restaurant tables and around desk legs. I would have to visualize how my leg was caught in order to move it in the correct direction to free it. It was odd sleeping at night; I couldn't tell whether my right leg and foot were under the sheets, on top of the sheets, tangled in the sheets, or even hanging off the bed. All of these symptoms and scenarios remain today, but I've learned to live with it and adapt.

My desire to get out of the hospital, return to work, and continue my life as usual was kind of typical for me. In fact, often I felt this was my curse in life—to have the kind of personality that refused to acknowledge any weakness or accept any support. Still, I often felt I received less credit than I deserved for overcoming the "fights" I'd had throughout my lifetime: fights to create a life for myself, fights to start and maintain and grow a business, fights to be the kind of man I wanted to be and have the kind of family life I dreamed of. I didn't want sympathy, but there were times when, truth be told, I wanted to feel acknowledged for what I'd gone through. By and large, I'd always received a lot of "OK, he's back. Move on."

Because I was back behind my office desk after my surgery, because I was out walking, because I was doing the normal things I'd always done, everyone, doctors included, commented on my "quick recovery." I soon discovered, though, that along with their congratulations, they were also making the assumption that I was *fully* recovered already. Because I was walking around my office, making decisions, reviewing appraisals, and getting back to business, people assumed, "Jay's OK," or, "Jay's back to normal."

Some people did understand the enormity of what I was facing. Allan and Jessica were constantly asking, "Do you want me to pick up some lunch for you?" or, "Hey, I'm going out, do you want anything to drink?" Plus, they served as buffers from any disgruntled clients or frustrated employees of the variety associated with any typical business day.

My family knew I wasn't completely back to normal. They knew how hard I was working every day and night just to fight off the relentless fatigue and deal with the nearly constant residual pain, not to mention painstakingly trying to adapt my brain and my legs to work better together—just to walk down the street.

I always had to play the tough guy, to work through things on my own without help from anyone. I'm sure that Lyn wished at times that I wasn't so hell-bent on proving I was a human Timex watch—someone who could "take a licking and keep on ticking" without missing a minute (OK, at least not beyond those seven days) of work. I know for a fact that I caused her more worry than I should have and sometimes—hell, a lot of times—probably pissed her off. She had reason.

Chapter 13
Worth the Risk

THE SECOND WEEKEND FOLLOWING THE SURGERY—
we're talking fewer than fourteen days out from when my skull
was pried open—my uncle, Jerry, and I went to look at some
midcentury furniture for BOA Antiques.

The opportunity to pick up some solid pieces of this type
of popular furniture, in good condition, no less, was too much
to pass up. We could usually sell this type of furniture at a very
nice profit. So, that weekend, with my uncle in town, I was
ready to drive off, check out the furniture, make an offer, and—
hopefully, if everything went well—load up a few pieces in my
truck and take them back to BOA, where Lyn was manning the
store.

Lyn was concerned. "Are you sure you are up for this, Jay?"
she asked.

"Of course. A few pieces of furniture is no big deal. Hey, if there's a couch, I'll take a nap." I joked as I usually do, trying to get her to relax.

Lyn was not amused. "OK, Jay. It's fine if you go, as long as you promise me one thing."

"What's that?"

"Remember," she said, "you still aren't supposed to be lifting anything heavy."

"I know, I know," I told her as I climbed into my truck, having already anticipated her concern. "But someone else will be there, and he and Jerry can load everything into the truck." She seemed satisfied, and Jerry and I took off.

The furnishings in the house we were visiting were in immaculate condition, and I knew several pieces would make great finds for our customers, many of whom were regulars. My uncle and I decided on three pieces of furniture, including a buffet cabinet. I knew Lyn would be thrilled with them.

There was only one problem. My uncle and I were the only ones who could load the items of furniture into the back of my pickup truck. I hesitated for about a half second. Lyn had warned me not to lift anything heavy, and these suckers—built by midcentury craftsmen and built to last—were cumbersome and very heavy. But they were also too fabulous to leave behind. Someone else would come along and scoop them up before we could get back with an extra pair of hands. We absolutely had to take them now.

So Jerry and I spent the next hour pushing and pulling and lifting, and we hauled three large, unwieldy (but beautiful) items of furniture out of the house. We had to finagle them— carefully!—down a rather steeply sloping driveway, and then wrangle them up into the back of my truck. I was dripping from the heat, and so was Jerry. He kept asking me, "You OK?"

"Fine," I'd grunt in response, but in fact, I did wonder a couple of times if I was pushing myself too much. But I didn't feel any throbbing in my head, and to be honest, it just felt good to be doing something normal like moving furniture. On our way back to the store, we debated what to tell Lyn. In the end, we didn't have to tell her anything.

As we pulled into the parking lot of our antiques store, Lyn came outside to greet us. As we were unhooking the ties that held the furniture in place, she looked over the furniture and said, "Wow, these are nice!" She started to say something more about their quality, but then stopped suddenly and turned to Jerry.

"Jay helped move these, didn't he?" she demanded. Jerry didn't respond; he just looked over at me, and she turned back to face me. I kept my mouth shut. Then she looked back at Jerry, obviously still waiting for an answer. But Jerry didn't give me up. And besides, Lyn already knew the answer to her question.

She was angry, I knew. But she let it go. By that time in our marriage, and certainly from what she'd seen in how I handled everything related to my brain tumor and surgery and going back to work so soon, she had become a bit resigned to my continuous "Mr. Tough Guy" act. She understood that I did it out of concern for her and our family. I wanted to keep them from worrying, to convince her and the kids that everything was all right.

Chapter 14

The Man in the Plastic Mask

I WAS SITTING IN MY OFFICE AND TALKING with Tom about his appraisal of a subdivision when I felt the all-too-familiar light-headedness and slight disorientation. "I have to go to the bathroom," I told Tom, which was true. I rushed to a stall in the men's room, took a seat on the lid of a commode, and put my head in my hands. I just needed a moment to regain my balance and recover my normality.

The light-headedness and imbalance were side effects of my radiation treatments. The radiation was to kill off any remaining tumor cells that might have been lingering postsurgery.

My neurosurgeon indicated that the radiation treatments should start about one month after my surgery; however, my wife and I had already planned a trip to Disneyland with the kids during the Christmas holiday. Therefore, my surgeon suggested we start radiation at the beginning of the new year in

2006. I was fine with putting radiation off until after my family vacation; my only question to my doctor was, "Am I clear to ride the roller coasters?"

The nurse in my neurosurgeon's office replied, "Dr. Nakaji said this is an odd request but said to tell you to take your vacation and go ahead and ride roller coasters . . . assuming, if you have *any* discomfort or headaches, you will stay off any fast or jolting rides!" That was all I needed to hear.

Since Briana, Adam, and Olivia were fourteen, thirteen, and twelve years old, respectively, we weren't planning on wasting time on the Snow White, Peter Pan, or Pinocchio rides. No, for this family vacation, we were going for the "big kids" rides—we would be riding the Matterhorn, Space Mountain, and everything "fast and furious."

I actually had more trouble getting to the rides than riding on them. I got tired several times as we all walked through the park. I struggled with my numb leg and sometimes my inability to keep my shoes on my feet. I had always been a total shorts-and-sandals, even flip-flops, kind of guy, and I continued to wear flip-flops as we toured Disneyland. Although I walked strangely, I managed to keep up with my family. I thought I was doing pretty well, until Briana held one of the flip-flops up to my face and said, "Missing anything, Dad?"

As it turned out, I couldn't feel anything on my right foot, and as I limped along, my flip-flop inevitably fell off. I just kept walking, doing my own one-foot impression of Shoeless Joe Jackson.

It didn't take long before I bought sandals that strapped across my feet, and I made sure to wear them, particularly on all the crazy thrill rides. Otherwise, a shoe would certainly have been seen flying from Space Mountain.

Still, I rode every roller coaster and thrill ride I normally would have ridden back in the days before BS (brain surgery). At times, truthfully, I was concerned about the possible damage I might be doing to my brain. Sometimes, as we stood in a line waiting for our turn on the newest, fastest, state-of-the-art thrill ride, I'd find myself wondering if all the whiplash-inducing tossing and high-speed roller coaster rides would somehow permanently scramble my brain. Each time that thought entered my head, I'd consider it for about a half second, then realize that I was an idiot for entertaining such a thought. Maybe my attitude was my way of avoiding considering the seriousness of my condition. I just felt that it was better for me to think positively and act normally unless something serious came up. Worrying about my condition would only make it worse. Joking about my condition and doing everything I wanted to do would improve my condition. Whatever the reason, during our family vacation I rode every (fast) ride possible.

My brain had survived a tumor the size of a plum; it had survived open-skull surgery; it could surely survive something from Disney.

Despite my one-shoed antics and some fatigue I had to fight off, my wife and the kids and I had a great vacation at Disneyland; we'd been through so much the entire previous year, it was an incredible relief and joy, really, to get away from all the medical "stuff" that had consumed our lives for so long.

But it wasn't all over. Not by a long shot.

After I returned from Disneyland with my strap-on sandals, I had to face the truth: five weeks of daily radiation, which is not just about radiation. Not only did I have to go in to a clinic every day, but also I had to have regular MRIs and meetings with my radiologist the entire five weeks as well. And if that doesn't sound like enough fun, well, I had to put a mask over my face every day as I underwent the ordeal.

Not everyone who undergoes radiation therapy has to wear a mask. However, my radiation was so precise, with seven different beams of radiation directed toward specific areas in the brain, that my head had to remain completely motionless so none of the beams would be misdirected.

These masks don't come off the shelf. They created my mask by heating the unformed plastic to make it malleable and then fitting it over my face to create a mold. Once the mask cooled, of course, it was something I had to wear for at least an hour every day for the next month and a half. In my case, the mask had a mesh design to allow breathing, and it was essentially bolted down over my face and onto the gurney I was lying on each time I had radiation treatment—to prevent even the slightest movement of my head. You can imagine how annoying this was for me, the guy who refused any help.

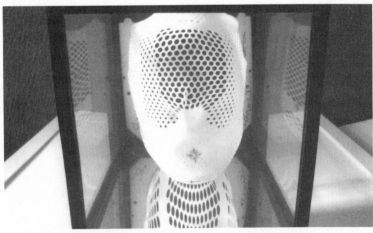

My mask in its homemade shrine

Chapter 15

Radiation Treatment

FIVE DAYS A WEEK, AT EIGHT O'CLOCK in the morning, over a five-week period, I went to the radiologist's office to get my daily dose. I'd requested an 8:00 a.m. appointment so I could head straight from radiation to my office every weekday. I was usually out by 8:30 or 8:45 a.m., and back in my office somewhere around 9:00.

I usually sat in the lobby, waiting with the same people. The lobby was quaint, yet inviting. A large tank in the center of the room was filled with exotic fish. At first, I took a seat in the front row; all the better, I thought, for getting in and out as quickly as possible. My front-row seat ritual came to a screeching halt, however, after the day a woman entered the lobby accompanied by her daughter, whom I guessed to be about six years old, and they sat in the two seats directly behind me. After a few minutes, I heard the little girl whisper to her mother—in that special "little kid" voice that they think is a whisper but is really quite loud—"Mommy, why does that man have a big cut in his head?" The mom quickly tried to hush her daughter, but I got the message.

With the oversized staples holding the skin on my skull tautly together, I was practically channeling Frankenstein, and I knew it. Though I downplayed any discomfort about how my head looked, I was somewhat embarrassed by it. I had been shaven somewhat for surgery, of course, and the radiation wasn't doing anything to help my hair grow back. Best not to scare little girls and their mothers. So, after that, I took my cue and sat in the back row, where no one would sit behind me and have to see the angry-looking sutures that stretched across five inches of my head.

Lyn accompanied me to the first few treatments, but eventually I told her it wasn't necessary. It wasn't like she could come in with me during radiation—no one but patients were allowed "behind the scenes," where the actual treatment took place, and for her to sit in the lobby thumbing through months-old, dog-eared magazines while I was in for treatment, and then for us to have to part ways as I went on to my office afterward, seemed silly. So, after the first few visits, she reluctantly stayed home and let me go on by myself.

Which suited me fine, really, and allowed me to indulge my hobby of people watching. The other patients I'd see every day waiting, like me, in the lobby, were old and young and every age in between, but all of them were weak. Most had a companion who drove them to their treatments and waited with them; I figured this was due either to their weakness or possibly depression. One older gentleman, whom I saw every day, was having treatment for throat cancer. His voice was merely a whisper and he was constantly coughing and spitting. I spoke with his wife a few times, but after a while they both stopped coming in. Later, I learned that his symptoms had worsened and he no longer could even make it in for the radiation treatments.

One day a young girl was wheeled into the lobby in a wheelchair. She was hairless, with a scarf tied around her head, and was wearing her pajamas. I would guess she was no more than seven years old. I spoke with her briefly as her parents checked her in at the front desk, and we exchanged radiation stories. She cringed as I told her about my mask, which she found to be much more excruciating than her treatments. But she was excited because she was finally nearing the end of her treatments. It was hard to keep the emotion I felt for this strong young girl from showing. She had her entire life ahead of her and was missing out on just being a kid. After we chatted, I sat there watching her interact with her parents. I was conscious of being in my dress clothes, as opposed to pajamas, and felt acutely aware of how fortunate and blessed I was to be relatively healthy postsurgery, knowing that even if I didn't feel that great after the radiation, I'd still be strong enough to go to work. I didn't feel sorry for her—she didn't deserve or need anyone's pity—but if I could have, I would have taken her place in an instant. I just wanted to shield her from all that she was going through and let her be a little girl.

In the waiting room, I would also periodically cross paths with Brenda, a friend of Lyn's whose son and daughter, Matthew and Jenna, were childhood friends with Adam and Olivia.

Brenda was receiving her second treatment of radiation for breast cancer, and we often sat in the lobby of the radiation department together. She was always very upbeat despite the fact that apparently the cancer had spread, and this second go-round of radiation was focused on a different part of her body. We spoke very specifically about our illnesses: the symptoms and the consequences. Though we didn't know it at the time, Brenda would unfortunately face a third round of radiation treatments in 2010. She is truly a fighter.

Oftentimes, "others"—those who are not ill—will avoid at all costs such conversations with people who are sick. "Others" seem to assume that a sick person would rather not talk about his or her illness. Or maybe they simply just don't have a clue as to what to say, what questions to ask, or just how to talk with a person who may be facing the biggest health battle of a lifetime. I always spoke quite openly about what I was going through— perhaps a bit too openly. For example, when I would describe the tumor as a "big bloody mess" and start to describe the gory details of the surgery or post-op treatments, it was frequently apparent that others wanted very much to avoid hearing any specifics. I guess it's human nature not to want to have to face the realities of a body that is sick or possibly dying. I guess it's less anxiety-inducing not to think about how or why someone is sick, because then you don't have to worry about whether the same thing could happen to you. This avoidance may also have been one of the reasons I insisted upon doing things my own way and not telling other people about my condition.

But believe me: the people who are ill, the ones who are sick fighting cancer or waiting for surgery or just recovering from surgery—they're "living" their illness every moment of every day. Most of the sick people I met along the way during my treatment exhibited a desire to talk about as much of what they were going through as anyone would be willing to listen to.

I was lucky enough to have a family who would listen to my vivid (sometimes too vivid) blow-by-blows of what I was going through, but a lot of sick people I got to know had no one to really listen to them.

So now, whenever I'm around someone who has had surgery or who has cancer, I ask a lot questions. Then I shut up and just listen. The large majority of the time, they seem to truly appreciate my earnest interest in the particulars of their condition.

That was one good thing about being in the waiting room with other people who were going through what I was going through—for the most part, we all felt comfortable sharing our stories, and most of the time, we really got what someone else was saying. As my own treatment neared completion, I knew I'd miss some of that instinctive understanding, that camaraderie, even when we differed in our approaches and feelings about the challenges we faced. They never judged. They had no idea who I was, nor how I was handling my scenario. But they were interested. Not because it had an impact on their career, not because I was a friend or family member, and not because they would even know me long enough after the illness was over, but merely because they were going through it as well—simply that one common bond.

My ordeal really started when I went in for the treatment itself. I lay down on a gurney. The nurse took the plastic/mesh mask, placed it over my face, and bolted it to the gurney. It held my head in place so that it wouldn't move.

If I had been claustrophobic, the mask would have been my worst nightmare. It was so formfitting that every time I blinked, my eyelashes would brush against the mask's interior and I'd realize just how closed-in my face was. Each time the staff placed the mask over my head, I'd be thinking, "What if I have a runny nose?" or "What if my nose itches?"

I made the mistake of asking the nurses how other patients dealt with this restraint, how they coped with having a mask that rendered them immobile for the better part of an hour, and quickly realized I'd opened up a can of worms. The nurses regaled me with story after story of patients who'd been so unnerved by wearing the mask, they'd begun screaming, "Let me out! Let me out!" Others would demand to be drugged up with Valium, Xanax, or the like before treatment. Fortunately, despite these horror stories, I rather quickly acclimated to wearing the mask restraint and would often surprise the nursing staff by completely nodding off during treatment.

I actually got to like the mask. I've heard that many radiation patients throw away their masks when their treatment ends, or they simply leave the masks behind at their radiologist's office after their last session. No way I was leaving mine behind. One day I went ahead and asked, "When the treatment is over, can I keep my mask?"

My question surprised the nurse, but she took it in stride: "Yours is the only face which will fit into it . . . it's yours." And so the mask came home with me and has been enshrined ever since on a pedestal under a plastic casement in my house. What to some might be a too painful reminder of the hard times, fear, and physical discomfort of radiation treatment was for me a symbol of success. It surely didn't belong in the trash.

After each treatment, I felt a small success and would count down the days I had left. I got a break every Saturday and Sunday but would start up again every Monday morning. After every treatment I eagerly drove to the office.

Chapter 16
The Biker Appraisers

OVER THE FIVE-WEEK TREATMENT PERIOD, I didn't miss a day of work. Nearly two weeks into treatment, right on time according to the schedule my radiologist predicted, my hair started falling out. It became fairly evident one afternoon around 4:00, at the office, when I grasped a clump of hair and, with a mild tug, pulled it right out of my scalp. Jessica was in my office as I performed this magic trick, and though I'm sure she was a bit more shocked than she let on, she just mildly asked, "Are you sure you want to do that?"

"Why, is there a big bald spot there now?" I asked.

She hesitated, obviously debating what the correct answer was, and finally, very timidly, said, "No, not at all, you can barely tell."

Jessica had been with the company for about three years. She was twenty-five, and very loyal. She was a very good liar, too. But not quite good enough. I knew what I had to do. I told her I was going to shave my entire head that night at home. And I went home and did just that.

The next morning I arrived back at the office, slick-headed and figuring I was a ringer for the actor Vin Diesel or the wrestler-turned-actor known as The Rock.

But I was far from it, really: With my newly bald head, the large scar that stretched across my concave skull was more prominent than ever. I was very self-conscious—way more than my bravado the previous day would have suggested. My self-consciousness might have been a result of the fact that I couldn't pretend I didn't have a bald head. Burying myself in work, learning to walk on my own, being independent would not hide the fact that I had lost my hair. I figured I had weeks ahead of me of feeling like I looked like crap before I'd grow accustomed to my new look.

I couldn't have been more stunned later that afternoon when eight of the male appraisers in my office, many of whom had worked with me for years, strolled into my office, one by one, each one sporting a completely bald pate. Apparently they had all been secretly planning this show of support for weeks— they were just waiting for the day, the inevitable day, when my hair would finally start to fall out.

The gesture was unbelievable to me. These eight men stood in my office, completely bald and with total disregard for how they looked. They didn't care how their wives and kids felt they looked; they were unconcerned with how clients would perceive their appearance. They didn't give a rat's ass what anybody else thought. Except me, of course. They wanted me to know, 100 percent, that they were there for me.

Don't Mess With Appraisers!

I will remember that moment for the rest of my life. Each one of them stood in front of me as an incredible example of what it means to "take one for the team."

We decided to capture this powerful gesture of solidarity before anyone's hair started growing back in.

I had the resulting photograph blown up and hung in an oversize frame for my office, where it still hangs. To this day, when new business clients or professional colleagues visit my office, the first question they ask me is, "Who are the bikers?" Or maybe, "Did you guys do this as a joke or for fun?"

I always give the same responses: "Not bikers . . . just very serious appraisers," "No, it definitely wasn't a joke," and "Yes, it was a lot of fun." That's the end of story for the visitors. My appraisal team is already known as among the best in Arizona;

no need to reveal them for the heroic personal friends they are underneath that outstanding professional reputation. They'd find that far more embarrassing than a bald head.

Chapter 17

The Big Boys of Little League

BY THE TIME I FINISHED MY RADIATION treatment, baseball season was about to begin. I was excited about getting back to coaching. I missed working with the kids and helping my stepson Adam develop into a responsible young man.

Our team during the spring/summer 2006 season was called the Longhorns, which hearkened back to my alma mater, the University of Texas (where I'd graduated with a BA in business administration; my master's came from Baylor). It was my second year coaching Adam in the Clarendon league, an inner-city Little League covering central Phoenix, and in many ways, this season would turn out to be an eye-opening teaching experience not just for the team but for me and my family as well.

At the beginning of the season, one day after the Junior

tryouts (for boys ages thirteen, fourteen, and fifteen) had wrapped up, I was walking across the baseball field after returning the baseballs we'd used during tryouts to a secure closet in the snack bar when Adam ran to catch up with me and told me that he had just seen one of the boys from the tryout grab Adam's bag and bolt off the field. The bag contained all of Adam's things—his glove, bats, cleats, and more. Adam pointed in the direction where the boy had headed with the bag, and we sprinted across the field to try to find him.

Just as we reached the street, we spotted a black sedan pulling away. I darted into the street and put myself directly in front of the vehicle so that it had to stop, which it did. The young woman in the driver's seat rolled her window down.

"Can I help you?" she asked.

"It seems one of the players in your car took my son's bat bag," I said.

"Is this true?" the woman asked as she turned to look at the three boys sitting in the backseat.

"No, we don't have it," the largest of the three boys said flatly.

"I think you do," I said in response. "You may want to look around the car again."

"No, we don't have it, Coach; sorry," he said, looking me straight in the eye with no expression while the other two boys looked away without saying a word.

Apparently thinking the matter was settled, the woman began to drive away, but as she did, I glanced at Adam. He was giving me a look that said, "They've definitely got it."

I trusted Adam and put my hand on the car, stopping it for the second time. I bent down and looked into the backseat at the two boys who had looked away earlier. I said firmly, "I need one of you to look around the car for a black bat bag."

And one of the boys turned, reached into the area behind their seat, and lifted Adam's black bag out, handing it over to me through the window.

"Sorry, Coach," he said, and the woman drove off without another word exchanged.

One week later, I would draft all three of those boys onto the Longhorns. The large boy, Alan—who I believe was the culprit who lifted Adam's bag in the first place—was my number one draft pick. I was fully aware that the two other coaches making selections during the tryouts had steered clear of these three boys during the draft. The boys were known to have come from a different, "troubled" league that was merging with the Clarendon league that year. Many parents and coaches did not look upon the merger of the leagues favorably.

These new boys were unknowns, and the other coaches chose to select regular Clarendon league players whom they had coached in previous years. That suited me fine. I'd watched the boys closely during tryouts and had seen the raw talent they exhibited, and I knew they possessed the potential to be even better. Because the other coaches passed them over, I was able to nab all three of them—Alan, Angel, and Emmanuel (or, as we came to call him later, "E-man")—as my first three choices during the draft. I'm sure the coaches thought I was crazy, and maybe I was, a little bit. After all, these kids, or at least one of them, had tried to run off with Adam's bag . . . who knew what other behavior could lie ahead?

If those three boys did have any problems, I wasn't about to deny them the chance to sort them out on the playing field over the course of endless practices, the pressures of games, and the competitiveness of pursuing a championship.

Of course, neither the coaches nor the boys knew any of that, and later, at our first practice, E-man asked, "Coach, why'd you pick us, after what we did?"

"I owe someone a second chance," I told him. He just looked at me kind of funny and said, "I don't know what the hell you're talkin' 'bout, Coach."

We began practices. As with the Yankees, we worked on collegiate-level drills but again incorporated fun diversions. I ran practices by myself until a few assistant coaches volunteered to help me near midseason. Rather than just run my players, our running drills always involved a baseball skill, such as taking the correct angle when rounding first base or picking up the third base coach when rounding second base. Although I believe strongly in fitness, I already had some "attitudes" on the team, and just making them run wasn't going to make them believe in me as a coach.

During the first season with the Longhorns, Alan showed up for every game, but we would never know whether Alan was high or not. As the season progressed, other players and I could usually determine Alan's state. Around the middle of the season, I gave Alan a mandate: show up sober or don't play. Some of the other players actually preferred dealing with Alan when he was high, as he was quiet and less violent. In any case, I never had to enforce the mandate. Surprisingly, Alan never again showed up high for a game, as far as I could tell. If I wasn't sure, I would ask other players; every time, their response was, "Coach, he's clean . . . it's hard to believe, but he's clean." This scenario lasted the duration of the Longhorns season and for the entire following season as well.

Yet Alan remained unpredictable.

At a particular practice, Alan remained belligerent and disrespectful throughout the drills. He was harassing other players, he was screwing around, and, most important, he was repeatedly ignoring me when I told him to knock it off. Finally I'd had enough; I confronted him and gave him two options. He could remain at practice and work at the drills, or he could leave.

Under his breath, he sarcastically stammered and glared at me.

"Do you want to repeat that?" I asked.

He continued to glare at me.

"Alan, I'll give you another chance . . . why don't you repeat what you said to me?"

Without a response, he maintained his glare, consistent with his attitude pertaining to the black bag incident. "Is there something you need to say to me?" I asked.

On this day, and after putting up with his antics on numerous earlier occasions, I forced the confrontation. As I walked toward him, he looked straight into my eyes, and ultimately we stood toe to toe, face to face. Alan was the biggest guy on the team, and on a daily basis he used his size to push others around.

Yet on this day, Alan said, "Coach, I'll stay," and walked away. For a sixteen-year-old who wasn't attending high school (he had dropped out of school during the previous year) and who was reportedly involved in a variety of street activities, this baseball team was definitely a highlight. If he walked away from me for no other reason than to continue playing baseball, we were both better for it.

Afterward, players told me they had my back. This incident took place early in the season, and while Alan would continue to have his ups and downs, he and I seemed to have an understanding. I respected him as a player, and he respected me as a coach. One year after our final state tournament game, I would see Alan at an Arizona Diamondbacks game that Briana and I were attending. Surprisingly, he gave me a big hug in front of one of his friends and asked if we were ever going to form a club team.

Numerous other players added character to our team. At six feet tall and about 175 pounds, Freddy was an athletic specimen. While Freddy usually struck out one out of every three at bats, anytime the baseball was thrown within his wheelhouse, he would send the ball well beyond the outfield fence. As a result, he had a handful of home runs throughout the season. And while his swing, with little movement in his lower body, was certainly not technically sound, his arm strength alone provided power to the bat.

As I watched my players run the bases, I realized that I would never "run the bases" of my life the way I used to; I knew that. My hair was falling out, my right leg and foot were still numb and probably would remain so for the rest of my life . . . but I chose to focus on my next turn "at bat." I lived for that, actually.

Because I had so many supposedly simple things to relearn, I looked at each one of them as my turn at bat . . . and all I wanted was the opportunity to blast it out of the ballpark each and every time. And I lived to be an example for the young people on my team. I believe that you can teach only by example.

You have to talk the talk and walk the walk (even if you are limping). That is the way I taught my kids. If I told them to work hard, I worked harder myself. If I told them not to do drugs, I didn't do drugs myself. If I told them to set goals, I set goals for myself. I acted the same way in my business. I knew I could get respect as a leader only if I worked harder than anyone else in the company. My reports had to be more accurate, my attitude had to be more positive, and my results had to be better than anyone else's. And if things didn't go well with the business, I took the hardest fall and the most responsibility.

Although I focused on being a role model on the baseball practice field, that didn't make the process of learning how to walk any easier. Like any toddler, I went through a long period of trial and error, with lots of starts and stops along the way. I started my routine by trying to walk without stumbling. When I accomplished this, I added some challenges. I started to run. However, I couldn't take any sharp turns or step in a hole or on top of a rock, as my ankle would simply twist, turn, and snap. Therefore, I ran slowly and for short distances.

Stairs were the hardest. Lacking the ability to judge placement of my right foot on each step, I frequently missed a stair or stepped too far. The end result was a face-plant.

I even had to invent a new way of driving. Usually, we use our right foot to step on the accelerator or the brake. But my right foot was numb, so it was difficult to control.

One day, with Lyn in my truck beside me, I was backing out of a parking space at a shopping center. I naturally turned and looked out the rear window. Focused as I was, I was not only unable to find the brake pedal with my numb right foot, but also I managed to catch my right foot underneath the brake pedal. Since my foot was numb, I wasn't even sure what it was caught on, nor could I sense how to free it. The whole time I was mentally trying to process what was happening, my truck continued to roll backward. Finally, I got the bright idea to quit struggling with my right foot and use my left foot to slam on the brake. I brought the truck to a halt just inches from the wall of a building.

"You're not driving anymore," Lyn said.

"No, I think I'm on to something with this left-foot thing," I said. "I can learn to drive with two feet!" And I've been doing that ever since.

Our team kept practicing. Our season was going to be a tough one, but I had a feeling we could do well.

If it wasn't enough to try to keep up with the players, I had to worry about the dent in my skull.

Chapter 18

The Metal Plate

THE DENT IN MY SKULL WAS THE RESULT of a second surgery that I had at the very beginning of the season. I needed surgery to remove an infected bone flap in my skull. By this time, going into surgery was old hat for me, but that didn't mean that I liked it any better. Since the removal of the tumor, my skull had not healed correctly, and an infection surrounded the bone flap. The surgery lasted only a few hours this time and left me with a huge convex crater in my head (as if it didn't already look bad enough). The surgeon told me that they couldn't put the titanium plate over the hole until the area was fully healed, which would take about ninety days, and I would have to wait until June until I could go back into surgery and get my titanium toupee.

So, for three months, I had to walk around with a huge

dent in my head—my normally gorgeous bald head was, for quite some time, sporting a crater left by the removal of the infected bone and tissue. Nothing more than a thin layer of sagging skin covered the hole. If they had beauty contests for brain-tumor survivors, I'd have had a good chance of winning during that time.

My surgeon had warned me several times to be extremely careful about allowing my head to come into contact with anything during this time. I wasn't even supposed to touch the vulnerable area. He'd told me that if anything were to penetrate the thin covering of skin and reach my brain, I could possibly suffer brain damage. I didn't want him to worry one bit, so naturally, I didn't tell him about my plans to resume coaching for the spring/summer season of Little League, which I started just a few days after this surgery.

Less than seventy-two hours after the infected bone was removed, I was on a baseball field, coaching, with a baseball cap covering my dent. Lyn had strongly recommended that I wear a helmet in case I got hit in the head by an errant baseball, but I'd told her no way was that happening.

"You have got to be kidding me!" I said. "Those kids will laugh me off the field."

And besides, I explained, a baseball would have to fall directly from the sky and strike the top of my head, where the soft spot was, to do any damage. What were the chances of that happening?

You know, looking back, I can see that I put my wife through a lot of unnecessary worry, and maybe I did expose myself to risks that weren't entirely necessary or in keeping with my underlying responsibility to my family to keep myself healthy and alive. But over the previous year, I'd come as close to death as I had ever imagined I could, and I wasn't about to live my life in any half measure now. I was still dealing with the whole mess—the infection, the need for the titanium plate, a leg and foot that were still relearning to navigate the world. Couldn't I at least have some fun and just feel like a regular guy?

Lyn, to her everlasting credit, never pushed her worries onto me. She'd express a concern, encourage me to exercise caution, and then stand by me, whatever I decided to do.

It was almost too bizarre, then, when I tested at least her patience, if not her loyalty, the night I came home from the Longhorns' first team practice—just days after the infected bone was removed—and told her the following story.

My new team and I had been practicing already for a couple of hours and were nearing the end of that first workout together. We were practicing bunts; the assistant coach, Bill was pitching, and players were either surrounding the mound to field the bunts or waiting close to home plate to take their turn at bat. I was on the field, about twenty feet from the batter, calling instructions to him, when out of nowhere a twirling, flying bat came hurtling toward me through the air. Unbelievably, it struck me smack in the head.

I wasn't knocked down, but I was dazed and dizzy.

Even in my woozy state, I demanded to know, "Where the hell did that come from?"

Every player on the field was aware of my condition, knew about the dent, and knew my head was sacred ground. To a man, they all froze in place.

In a flash, Bill was at my side. "Are you OK, Jay?" he cried. "Where did it hit you?"

I pointed to the top of my forehead, where there was now a small cut, maybe four or five inches away from my not-to-be-touched-under-any-circumstances dent.

I was regaining my equilibrium quickly and noticed Angel turn toward E-man. I heard Angel scream, "E-man, what the fuck?"

"It slipped out of my hands . . . I was just swinging the bat," E-man stammered.

I slowly reached down to pick up the dastardly bat, walked it over to E-man, and then held it out for him to take. He stood there, speechless and probably horrified by what he'd accidentally done. He eventually reached out and gingerly took the bat from my hand, and I walked back to the pitching mound.

"All right," I called. "Who's up next?"

I knew I'd have to tell Lyn all about it when I got home—truly, what were the odds of that happening?—and I could only imagine her reaction. But for now, I had to wrap up the first practice with my new team.

The Longhorns won the first two games of our season 11–10 and 7–6. Despite two games that easily could have resulted in losses, our team was starting to gel.

A couple of months later, in June, I went under the knife again for the insertion of a permanent, protective titanium plate between my skin and the top of my skull—for the purpose of covering the aforementioned crater the removal of the infected bone had left.

After both surgeries, while I was waiting to be released from my hospital recovery room, my neurosurgeon would stop in to check on me. He always told me my past recoveries were quick. Although I'd rather not have had any surgeries at all, the competitive part of my ego was at least gratified to hear that I was a quick healer. This proved to me that my attitude toward healing was the correct one.

After the second surgery, though, I saw the downside of being a fast healer when the doctor put in stitches to close my skin up instead of using staples as he had before. Within a few weeks, my scalp skin had completely grown over the stitches, which unfortunately caused problems when it came time to remove them.

"Well, we have two choices," Dr. Nakaji revealed. "We can numb your head and I'll have to cut the stitches free, or I can try pulling them out from under the skin. The second option may hurt."

I refused to take any painkiller and told the doc to just go ahead and yank 'em out. Dr. Nakaji knew me well enough by this time not to waste time trying to persuade me to accept novocaine. He just said, "OK," and then, with a pair of pliers (well, they looked like pliers), he proceeded to yank those stitches, one by one, out of the skin on my head. Because I'd asked for it that way, I didn't let out a peep, but boy, was he right; it hurt like hell.

Even if it wasn't the best idea to avoid painkillers, I was oddly proud of my "metal-head" status. I was actually a bit disappointed when I passed through airport security without tripping an alarm of some sort. Why weren't the alarms going bonkers? I was concealing metal in my head! I later learned that the type, material composition, and location in the body of the implant were all independent predictors of detection. Still, I was a bit concerned that I could bring a chunk of titanium onboard an aircraft.

Chapter 19

Baseball the Hard Way

AS THE ONLY BLACK PLAYER on the Longhorns, Freddy had earned the respect of his mostly Hispanic teammates, yet his family and personal life outside of baseball constituted an uphill battle. During the 2006 season, baseball was one of the most positive influences in Freddy's life. He lived with his mom, his younger brother, and his aunt Lalah, who was only fifteen years old, or less than one year older than Freddy. Lalah's mother had died the year before, from causes I never learned anything about, and Freddy's mom had brought Lalah to live with them. Lalah also played on our team, which was co-ed.

In order to show up, Freddy and Lalah would ride more than ten miles on a city bus to reach our practice field. Freddy always showed up, and always on time. Some days his afro would be pushing the baseball cap up off his head; other days he wore cornrows. He never let up in practice, improving his athletic ability enough over time to earn himself a starting position in an extremely competitive lineup.

"I got *skeels*," Freddy would say, dragging out the vowel for emphasis.

To develop the "skeels" of the team as a whole, I did my best to add creativity to the mundane nature of practicing baseball day after day after day, and to develop memories our players could share with one another throughout the season.

We had annual Wiffle ball games. A Wiffle ball is a baseball-size plastic ball with holes in it, disallowing it from being thrown very hard, yet enabling it to rise, drop, or curve in all directions. Regardless of how hard the ball was hit with its plastic bat, it rarely traveled beyond the infield. I would designate two players as captains—usually the two with the least talent, to keep them from being picked last. They would take turns choosing players. Not surprisingly, these games were extremely competitive, and the players were still practicing baseball fundamentals, even though they didn't realize it. As the umpire, I was always offered some sort of bribe, such as, "Coach, I'll give you a dollar if you don't call me out." I told them the price was a lot higher than one dollar.

At least once a year, on a particularly hot day, Lyn and I would fill sixty or seventy water balloons and I would take them to practice. I'd keep the balloons hidden in my truck until practice was over. The first time I introduced water balloons, I learned quickly that I was not exempt from being drilled and completely soaked. Consequently, on subsequent occasions I would arm myself with at least two or three water balloons.

These water balloons would hit me anywhere on my body (although the rule was to avoid anyone's head), at a speed of 50 to 60 miles per hour—essentially as hard as they could throw.

With people running all over the field and water-filled balloons flying all over the place, I would unload the few balloons I had, making sure I could score direct hits that would completely soak my target. Just when I thought all of the balloons were tossed and none of us could possibly be more drenched, I would see Jonathan out of the corner of my eye, holding one remaining balloon. Unfortunately, that balloon had my name all over it, and not a single word or threat I could say would deter Jonathan. So . . . I just started running, to at least deflect the blow. Yet, the blow was inevitable and took place with the entire team cheering for Jonathan. The only words of encouragement my players offered to me were, "Coach, you better get your ass running!" Overall, both Wiffle ball and the water balloons provided ample memories and a few bruises.

Throughout the summer of 2006, I continued sporting my Vin Diesel look, shaving what was left of the hair on my head on a regular basis. So many hair follicles were killed by the radiation that it just made sense to keep "the look" going. Fortunately, when you're living, breathing, and practically eating baseball with a bunch of teenage boys month after month, you end up wearing a baseball cap nearly 100 percent of the time anyway. That worked fine for me. Being bald left me no other way to cover the ghastly, five-inch scar across the back of my skull, which had become only more obvious and glaring from being opened and closed four more times during the two subsequent surgeries for the infection and to insert the titanium plate.

With my baseball cap on, the scar was hidden, for the most part; except for when the national anthem was being played before the start of a game, I rarely took it off. The team members and I were able to focus on baseball, not my brains (thank God), and they rarely mentioned anything about my condition. I didn't bring it up, either, unless it was absolutely necessary.

Of course, as with any life-threatening surgery and follow-up treatments, consequences continue throughout the duration of your life; in my case these consequences include lifelong antiseizure medication, subsequent brain scans, MRIs, doctor visits, and a lot more. Consequently, as much as I tried to keep my personal life separate from our time on the baseball field, many of my players shared the entire experience.

Jay's new hair style . . . Lyn's is much better

Chapter 20

Learning from My Players

ON GAME DAYS DURING THE REGULAR SEASON, all of my players would meet at the practice field—some arriving via bicycle or bus, others getting dropped off by a family member or friend, and still others actually walking the distance. Few, if any, parents attended our games; we didn't have interested parents who would volunteer to carpool or caravan to help transport the team to away games. To avoid forfeiting these games, I decided to rent a fifteen-passenger van to carry us to the ball field together.

After games, Lyn, who attended all of our games, and I would drop the players off back at our practice field, from which they'd return home the same way they came. But for Freddy, who took the bus, night games ended after the city buses stopped running. So Lyn and I got into the habit of dropping the rest of the team at the field and then chauffeuring Freddy, and often Lalah if she attended practice, to their front door.

During the half-hour drive, with just me, Lyn, Adam, and sometimes Briana and Olivia in the van, Freddy would reveal numerous aspects of his life. Sometimes his aunt Lalah was in the van too, and she'd chime in, but it was mostly Freddy's time to talk. He'd tell us about the financial struggles his family was going through (on several occasions we sent money home with Freddy to help buy groceries or cover rent), the violence in his neighborhood, the gang fights between Hispanics and blacks at his school, and the endless stories of relatives of his who were in prison.

In spite of what appeared to have developed into a close relationship between Freddy, me, and my family, he remained guarded.

"My family is tight," Freddy would boast.

"So, where is your dad?" I would ask. "Do you know him?"

"Nah, he's not around no more."

"Where is he?"

"Don't know," Freddy would respond, and then change the subject back to baseball.

Though at times he would reveal himself as emotionally vulnerable to circumstances in his personal life, he would quickly raise his walls back up and return to the arrogant and confident mask he most often wore. He obviously had learned in life to rely on no one and never to allow anyone to get too close.

Baseball was clearly Freddy's outlet, and one that allowed him to express positive qualities. From what we'd heard, he was feared at school, and when he felt threatened, he fought, on some occasions hospitalizing those who challenged him.

Freddy and Adam attended the same high school. Once, in Adam's freshman year, he was attending a school dance and inadvertently stepped on the foot of a very large, older, black, female student. Adam had been hanging out with friends, goofing around a bit, and simply stumbled and landed one of his feet squarely on one of the girl's—who likely outweighed Adam, then a very skinny fourteen-year-old, by about 50 pounds.

When Adam's foot made contact with hers, she screamed bloody murder. "I'm gonna kick your skinny white ass!" she yelled as she stormed toward Adam, who at that point had moved away a bit.

Adam was in a quandary in the microseconds he had to process the situation. He was raised to believe that it was never OK to hit a girl, no matter the circumstances, but she was barreling toward him like a freight train. Adam froze like a deer in headlights as he tried to figure out what to do.

Just as the girl started to place her hands on Adam's throat, Freddy appeared on the scene and stepped in.

"Bitch, leave my friend alone!" Freddy shouted, which stopped her in her tracks. Obviously confused, she said, skeptically, "This white boy is your *friend?*"

"Yeah," Freddy said. "He's my friend, so leave him alone!"

Enough said; Adam was spared the girl's threatened asskicking and thereafter enjoyed a new reputation as Freddy's friend.

The most instrumental player on the team was Jonathan.

Jonathan was quiet and intimidating, without question the best pitcher in the league. When my team had faced him the previous season, his presence on the mound daunted our players. He rarely spoke, just reserved a special glare for every player who stepped up to bat. Luckily for my team at that time, we rarely encountered Jonathan during games; he was often AWOL from the opposing team's lineup when game day arrived.

When I drafted Jonathan for the Longhorns in 2006, I was as surprised when the other two coaches ignored his talent as I had been when I drafted Alan, Angel, and E-man. I learned why they'd passed on him after I announced him as my next pick. One of the coaches, who'd evidently coached Jonathan before, turned to me and said, "Good luck getting Jonathan to show up . . . for practices or for games." I found out that we'd seen him so rarely at games because he had a track record of never showing up for practice and showing up for only about half of the regular-season games.

True to his past, Jonathan maintained his record once he was a Longhorn and would show up only randomly for practices. Yet, when he did bother to show up, he worked hard at the drills I'd set up. Almost in spite of his seeming indifference and erratic training, the new training program enhanced Jonathan's natural athletic ability, and his skills were improving. Jonathan was a natural-born competitor.

He was a serious asset for our team, and I tried to instill in him that it was all about the team. Once, early in the season, he missed the start of a game and didn't show up until we were already a few innings in. By that point, he'd already missed a couple of games altogether, so I put him on the bench through several innings. Toward the end of the game, however,

I relented and let him back into the lineup so he'd have one at bat and six outs in the field—as Little League rules require.

When his turn came, he stepped up to the plate, cool as a cucumber, and blasted a two-run home run, securing our team's victory by one run.

After the game, I clasped him on the back and said, "Jon, maybe you should start showing up on time for games." He just smiled at me, but for the rest of the season he was never late.

Chapter 21

Hanging Tough

THE LONGHORNS WERE UNDEFEATED after seven games and in the midst of a battle with another team, the Yankees, who did not like us, nor did they respect our record. We'd beaten them in a recent game, but just barely.

The rivalry came to a head one night when we once again faced off against the Yankees. We'd squeaked out the first win, and now the Yankees were bringing their "A" game.

It was proving to be an equal challenge for the two teams, but with the added drama of taunting among opposing players. Because the game was on the Yankees' home field, our fielders were also being heckled by Yankees' fans and players on the bench. When Angel, who played shortstop and pitched, hit a long drive down the left-field foul line, the umpire ruled it a home run, and the Yankees and their fans went ballistic. Next, their coach stormed the field, ranting and raving at the ump that the ball was clearly foul.

I was coaching third base, so I had had a fairly clear view of the home run shot—which definitely appeared to me to be foul, but the ump had made his call, and so I kept my peace and remained in my coaching box.

After ten minutes of chaos, the umpire threatened to toss the Yankees' coach out of the game and terminate the contest. So, finally, everyone calmed down and play resumed. We ended up winning the game by two runs, and we knew we would encounter some difficulty leaving the ballpark, as the taunting between the two teams had never ceased; in fact, it had only escalated.

I told our guys to pack up as quickly as possible and not to linger on the Yankees' home field whooping it up in celebration of the win. It didn't make much difference anyway, because despite our hurrying, we reached the parking lot and found the entire Yankees team waiting for us, bats in hand.

What started out as brawl-ready arrogance and confidence, though, slowly diminished to apprehension as their players were introduced to several of ours: Freddy, Alan, Angel, E-man, and Jonathan. These five players, who'd had little use for one another at the beginning of the season, had slowly formed a bond as the season progressed. There was no backing down by these Longhorns, who were taking a stand for one another and for the team, regardless of whose parking lot we were all standing in.

They weren't going to back down, but I sure wasn't about to stand by and let all hell break loose, either. Lyn, assistant coach Bill, and I began shoving our players into cars to avoid confrontation. However, this was one night I hadn't been able to reserve a rental van, and since few of our players' families attended our games, we didn't have enough vehicles for all of our players to leave quickly. A few parents, other family members, or friends were scheduled to come to the field to pick some of the Longhorns up, but they were late, so we were forced to wait in the parking lot.

We got players into the cars as quickly as we could, and we sent them off with instructions to go straight home. But just as quickly, I'd turn around and find them, out of the cars, standing in the parking lot, ready to rumble and practically daring the Yankees to swing just one bat. My players, of course, were empty-handed, since I'd grabbed every bat and secured it out of reach—they were empty-handed, but they'd never back down. Eventually, everyone got into cars and headed safely home. No physical fight ever broke out, but it was a very real, very tense situation. If my wife and I had had any illusions about what some of these boys were up against in their personal lives outside of baseball, that night was a stark reminder of just how close to the edge their physical safety could be.

The next time we played against the Yankees, it was at our home field, and there was no repeat of the earlier game's taunting and undertone of violence. We schooled them once again, beating them on the field, and afterward, they appeared to be somewhat humbled by the abilities of the now-proud Longhorns team, which, before the start of the season, had been just a hodgepodge group of ballplayers who had no reason to stand together as real teammates. Now, these guys were prepared to defend their team anywhere and anytime.

Chapter 22

A Nice Lull in the Action

DESPITE HAVING THE TWO SURGERIES to get rid of the infected bone flap and insert a titanium plate to cover the resulting hole in my head, the year 2006 was shaping up to be a good one.

Briana and Olivia were both active in beauty pageants during this time. In 2005, they both had won the crown, in different divisions, of "Miss Phoenix," which qualified them to advance to regional competitions in California.

We didn't take the pageant stuff too seriously throughout 2006, though it was a lot of fun for the girls, and for the people-watching—especially with some of the hyper "pageant moms" acting beyond hilarious.

My Little League team was littering playing fields with victory after victory, the tumor in my head was gone, my skull was healing, I could drive with two legs, and I was walking like a very talented eighth-grader.

I hadn't had a vacation with my family since December 2005, and in late summer 2006, we took a family trip. For several years, my family had enjoyed a tradition of planning our summer trips to a different U.S. city, where we'd attend a professional baseball game (naturally) and tour a university—where someday our kids might enroll. Our plan was to give them exposure to schools all over the country so they could see firsthand a variety of campus situations and have a better understanding of the opportunities available within large schools, small schools, private schools, and public schools, when it came time for them to make choices about where to go to college.

In previous years, we had visited Las Vegas, New Orleans, Denver, Seattle and New York City. In 2006 we decided to go to Boston, aka "Beantown," and, more important, the home of the legendary Red Sox. Naturally, we went to Fenway Park, visited the mythical outfield wall called the "Green Monster," and witnessed "Big Papi"—Sox batter David Ortiz—hit a walk-off home run in the bottom of the ninth inning to win a game against the Orioles.

Naturally, when we visited Boston, the first campus on our wish-list tour was Harvard University. The Crimson campus did not disappoint us. We also drove by the Massachusetts Institute of Technology, in addition to visiting the John F. Kennedy Presidential Library and eating at the original "Cheers" restaurant and bar.

We also walked, walked, and walked. If you've ever spent even a few hours in Boston proper, you know that walking—a lot of walking—is required. We walked everywhere, including the 2.5-mile-long Freedom Trail, a redbrick walking trail that winds among sixteen historically significant sites in the city.

As I walked through the city with my family, despite my fascination with all that we were seeing and learning, at times I'd find myself feeling light-headed and exhausted. I wasn't really sure if it related to everything my body had been through over the previous two years or if, because I'd been so much less active following my surgery and recuperation and had put on a few extra pounds in the process, I was feeling drained simply because I was overweight and out of condition. I never figured it out; I just sucked it up, kept my mouth shut, and kept walking. And walking.

When we returned to the hundred-degree-plus Arizona weather, things felt cool in comparison to Boston, where I wasn't used to the humidity, and as summer ended and fall began, life in general just seemed to be smooth.

Our antiques store continued to plug along, creating a modest cash flow. The only problem was that cash flow was dependent on Lyn being there. BOA Antiques had a great mom-and-pop reputation with regular buyers, which was great, but the downside was that our regulars wanted to shop and bargain and buy only when Lyn, whom they all liked very much, was in the store. That made it pretty hard to leave the store in the hands of part-time workers. In order to spend time with Lyn and help out as well, I would spend several hours each weekend at the store. Sometimes I'd review appraisal reports in the back office and just help if and when I was needed.

Periodically all three of our children would help out too, with inventory or at the register.

Still, the biggest thrill of the summer was our undefeated Little League team.

Chapter 23

Taking One for the Team

WHILE ALAN COULD DEFINITELY PROVOKE, he was often prejudged, as were several other players on the team. The reason, most likely, was their appearance. I was used to umpires informing me before each game that our players would need to remove their necklaces, earrings, and other jewelry (all of which were a bit unusual for Little League players, but they were a part of who our players were). Sometimes umpires also asked me if my players spoke English, based on their assumption that many of the players spoke only Spanish. However, I was outright shocked during one regular-season game when I "became one of them" and finally realized how they were occasionally treated.

We were playing a team we had played before, composed primarily of Caucasian players. They had a great coach and friendly players; in fact, although we had beaten them each time we faced each other, all players on both teams got along, and we always had a competitive game. In this particular game, a new umpire from their division (the game was at their home field) was in charge, and when the game became competitive in the fourth and fifth innings, he became very uncomfortable with the scenario. The other team was at bat, and the majority of their players were yelling from the dugout, encouraging their hitters. Our first baseman, Alan, started yelling to encourage our pitcher, Jonathan, and the umpire stopped the game. He called me out of the dugout, onto the field, to inform me that Alan would be thrown out of the game unless he stopped antagonizing their players. My response was that Alan was simply into the game, as were their players, and yelling in encouragement in the same fashion. At that, the umpire threatened to throw *me* out of the game unless I returned to my dugout. I pointed out that he, in fact, had called me out of the dugout and onto the field. The umpire did not receive this statement very well; he gave me a final warning. I walked back, slowly and quietly, to the dugout.

In between innings, the umpire went over to the opposing team's dugout and proceeded to tell their coaches that our team was ready to "rumble," and that I was instigating a brawl. As I stood in the coach's box along the third-base dugout, I could see that the opposing coaches found humor in what the umpire was saying. I should have let it go at this point, but at the end of the inning I approached the umpire to assure him I was not encouraging my players to fight.

Again, not a good idea. He gave me an ultimate warning to not speak to him again throughout the rest of the game, and he informed me that he would not allow my "delinquents" to come up to our opponents' home field and cause trouble. For a brief moment I considered a right blow to his face or maybe a knee to his balls; then I realized that he expected exactly that of me and my players. Therefore, I just walked away, mumbling, "what an ass." I hoped that he might hear me. He didn't.

I had finally become a true part of this team, having experienced the bias based on race, color, or perception to which these boys had, unfortunately, become accustomed. After the game, all my players joked and laughed about how I was almost tossed from the game; however, they had no idea how disturbed and shocked I was by the incident and how saddened I was by how some would prejudge not just them individually, but us as a team. We were one.

As our record of wins mounted, I continually reminded all my players how unique and difficult it is to complete an undefeated season in any sport, at any level.

"We are now the target," I commenced, "which means we not only have to play better, but we have to perform better."

"Coach, what's the difference?" Jonathan asked.

"Performing better is not just playing baseball better. It's working harder, improving our sportsmanship on and off the field, and conducting ourselves better. These teams can 'make' their entire season by beating us. They can become the *only* team to beat us. But if they can't beat us, they're going to want to get into your heads. They're going to harass you, antagonize you, and push all your buttons, only to get you to react, to respond, or to fight back. You have to be better. You have to maintain your composure, not trash-talk back, and walk away."

"Coach, we don't walk away from no one!" Alan stammered.

"Hell no, Coach," responded E-man.

"Yes we do," I continued. "We walk away winners. We walk away fighting our battle on the diamond and nowhere else. And we walk away with pride and with sportsmanship. Let's surprise the players, let's surprise their fans, and let's surprise the umpires. They'll be surprised that as good as we are on the diamond, we're not cocky, we play at a high level of sportsmanship, we don't trash-talk, and we don't argue calls from the umpires."

I got to know the team even better, especially Jonathan. When Lyn and I had decided to take the team to batting cages in lieu of regular field practice, a switchblade fell out of Jonathan's pocket as the boys were lining up to bat. I had heard something fall to the ground, and as I turned to see what it was, Jonathan reached down to scoop it up and said, "Sorry, Coach, you won't see that again at practice." When I asked him why he was even carrying a switchblade, he responded with his own question, "Why do you think, Coach?"

I let it go, content with his promise that he wouldn't "carry" while at practice. Later, I learned a lot more about his life. Over time, we formed a strong relationship that sometimes took the form of a father-son bond, other times a good friendship.

Coaching Angel and E-man could be accomplished only on a day-to-day basis. They would occasionally miss the team van for regular-season games, in which case they would sometimes show up on time, other times arrive after the game had started, and still other times not show up at all. As always, the consequence was limited playing time; however, Little League requires all players to have one at bat and to play in the field for six outs in every game. When Angel and E-man were "on," they played hard, motivated each other, and were leaders on the field. When they were "off," anything could happen.

We won our final regular-season game 18–5 over our most competitive rival; however, rather than end the season on a high, we had an incident in the van after the game. E-man was taunting his teammate Nikk in the back of the van, and comments, slaps, and slugs transpired before E-man eventually went over the seat and started a brawl with Nikk. Looking in the rearview mirror, I could see arms flailing. In the middle of a residential neighborhood, I had to pull the van over, jump out, and open the rear doors, as it was impossible for me to make my way through four rows of seats filled with players who were doing nothing but yelling and watching the fight progress.

As quickly as I rushed to the back of the van, so did Jonathan, also to help break up the fight. As usual, the only other adult in the van was Lyn, and there was no way she was going to move from the front passenger seat. Together, Jonathan and I pulled E-man off Nikk and out of the van; I spent the next five minutes yelling and holding E-man in an attempt to calm him down, with neighborhood residents watching. Afterward, the team joked about how they were certain E-man would start whaling on me. Although he appeared to be completely out of control, he eventually settled down. None of the residents called the police, or we got out of there before any law enforcement showed up. E-man was not necessarily a big teenager—he had braces and wore glasses—but the fire inside of him was evident that night.

Despite the occasional trouble, the team performed, for all practical purposes, nearly flawlessly, both as individuals and as a group. They were tremendously proud of their accomplishment, as they should have been. Going undefeated was no small feat for a team of players who mostly didn't know each other at the beginning and who had personal, financial, and family struggles to contend with throughout the season. I was proud just to be associated with them.

Typically, the Little League season ends with all-stars games. Because most of the Longhorns players were fifteen years old, they were ineligible to compete in the junior all-star program, which was limited to thirteen- and fourteen-year-olds. A senior level of all-star competition did not exist within the Clarendon league at that time; as a result, after we won and celebrated our final game of the season, I was uncertain if I would ever see any of these young players again.

Chapter 24

Taking the Time to Enjoy Life

THE END OF THE SEASON MEANT that I had extra time on my hands. Of course, as I've pointed out before, I can take only so much quiet. So that fall, somewhere along the line, I decided to become a playwright and stage director. Hey, why not?

Adam and Olivia were members of a small, nondenominational church in Phoenix that each year put on a Christmas play performed by youth members. I had watched the plays the previous two years and knew the church had struggled to find parents willing to put in the hours necessary to coordinate, rehearse, and produce the play. So I offered my services—despite the fact that I'd never pulled together a theatrical performance in my life. But I had seen plenty of movies and watched my kids in plenty of plays. I wanted to give the standard Christmas play a twist. How hard could it be?

Charity Brain Tumor "Walk"; Olivia (Left) & Briana (Right)

My play was entitled *The Christmas Choir Club* and was based on a combination of two movies I'd seen several times: *The Breakfast Club*, a 1980s teenage angst flick that had featured several young stars including Judd Nelson and Molly Ringwald, and *Sister Act*, the hilarious 1990s comedy featuring Whoopi Goldberg as a singing nun.

Despite the somewhat bizarre combination of movies upon which the play was based, and despite the fact that the performers had to sing, the kids seemed to have a lot of fun preparing and practicing for the play, and then performing it in front of the congregation. The play went over pretty well, and I believe the congregation enjoyed the deviation from the regular lineup to which they had been exposed year after year.

As for my company, by December it was clear that we were going to have a record year, and that for the fiscal year 2006 we would achieve gross revenues of approximately $2.6 million.

We had grown to a total of fifteen employees, and for the year-end Christmas party, I decided to take everyone not just out of town for a nice dinner, but out of state for a "What Happens in Vegas, Stays in Vegas" holiday excursion. I flew all my employees and their significant others to Las Vegas that December, and we celebrated our great year of success and the season of Christmas at the Mirage hotel and resort.

We had a blast in Vegas. As was our tradition, we roasted two longtime employees, in this instance Mark and Kevin, each of whom had been with the company for five years. I presented Mark with a blow-up sex doll—his midlife crisis mistress— and a Matchbox sports car—his midlife crisis car. Fortunately, Mark has a great marriage, and more important, he and his wife each have a great sense of humor. Since he was a huge baseball fan, I also gave him a thousand dollars' worth of Arizona Diamondbacks tickets.

Kevin was married for a second time and had three children, two from his first marriage and one from his second. He was a great husband and a wonderful father. So, naturally, my gift to him involved a hired actor of Asian descent, in his early twenties, who stormed into our meeting room at the Mirage claiming to be Kevin's long-lost illegitimate son—conceived while Kevin served overseas in the Navy Reserve.

Kevin stood up, gave the actor a big hug, and dramatically exclaimed, "Son, where have you been all these years?!" Kevin's real gift, though, was a tribute to his role as father—a thousand dollars' worth of "Disney dollars," which he would undoubtedly be able to put to good use with young children in the house.

After the roasts, we played a game of *Family Feud* that was equally embarrassing. Even though we played in the spirit of good-natured ribbing, it doesn't hurt that I have a fantastic team of good-humored colleagues and co-workers.

When Christmas actually arrived, I celebrated at home with my family. Needless to say, I was extremely grateful to have made it through all the drama of a year that began just after I'd been diagnosed and operated on for the first time. While I don't remember precisely all the gifts I received on Christmas morning 2006, I will always remember one that will touch my heart forever.

It was a music CD from Briana—in which she was doing the singing. The CD comprised two songs Al recorded at his studio in our antiques-store building. My talented daughter— and I'm not just saying that because I'm her dad—beautifully sang "Chestnuts Roasting on an Open Fire" and "Grown-up Christmas List." The latter is my all-time favorite Christmas song. To my ears, Briana's version sounded much better than the versions by Natalie Cole and Amy Grant.

There was also a message to me from Briana on the CD— spoken, not sung. And you'll just have to indulge a father and let me include the whole thing below.

Dad. There is not much else for me to say, besides the fact that I am who I am today because of you. I am so thankful that you are my dad. No one can compare to you. You inspire me with your determination and willpower and your immense love for others. You are constantly trying something new. Something that always seems to bring others just as much joy and excitement as it brings you. I am amazed at how you handle everything in your life with such ease. You teach me something new every day, whether it's in your actions or your inspiring words. You never cease to let me know that you care, and you have supported me so much throughout my life. I know I can always tell you what's on my mind, and that you'll never judge me; and that is a huge blessing and gift that I am constantly aware of. Thank you for everything you do, have done, and will do for me. I love you with all my heart, and my life would not be the same without you. You have taught me so much throughout these years, and I can't imagine what life will be like in a couple of years for me without your company or our conversations to comfort me when I need them the most. You are one of the only people that truly understand me inside and out. For I have come to see, more and more, that we are pretty close to being the same individual, and it's so good to know that God not only blessed me with someone like that in my life, but that someone is my dad. I love you. Merry Christmas.

Not many things bring tears to my eyes, but this CD, with these two songs and the incredible message from my daughter, is capable of doing just that. I had tears in my eyes that December 25, and they come back every time I listen to it. That's my daughter, I say to myself; she thinks she's blessed to have me for a dad, but I'm the one who's blessed.

Chapter 25

Ya Gotta Have Style

JONATHAN WAS THE FIRST PERSON to call me before the next Little League season to find out if he was going to be able to play. As a seventeen-year-old he was no longer eligible to play in the Junior league, and, as I've noted, the Clarendon league had not fielded a Senior team in many years. Consequently, when Jonathan found out we were forming a Senior team, all he wanted to know was, "When's the first practice, Coach?"

Our 2007 team consisted of two players, including Adam, whom I had coached for three years; two players whom I coached during the first and third years; and five players who had played for me the previous two years. Our record spanning the 2006 and 2007 seasons would end up at 23–3, including the undefeated 11–0 in 2006. However, we would again work hard through trials and tribulations to achieve the 23-win record. The request by players to continue playing ball and the lack of baseball beyond the Junior league within the Clarendon district were the impetus for the creation of a Senior team in 2007, in order for these same players not only to continue playing baseball, but also to qualify for all-stars and compete at a higher level. Notably, the Clarendon league had not fielded a Senior team within the previous decade, as most inner-city boys would lose interest by the time they reached fifteen or sixteen.

My first step was to serve on the Clarendon Little League board of directors so I could propose the formation of a Senior team. Most board members doubted that we could success- fully recruit fifteen- and sixteen-year-olds to play, arguing that they either lose interest at this age or shift to more competi- tive "club" ball because teenagers playing Little League was not "cool." In essence, the combination of these factors was the reason Clarendon had not fielded a Senior team in many years. Also, as part of a league with poor monetary support, most board members strongly felt what little money there was should be spent on the younger, more active divisions. At the Major level, which comprised ten- to twelve-year-olds, Clar- endon had four teams, totaling nearly sixty kids.

Before the 2007 season, the league checking account con- tained a few thousand dollars, all of which, and much more, was needed to support all teams ranging from the T-ball level to the Junior league. To help, I donated a thousand dollars from my business, I raised another thousand dollars from business spon- sors, and Bill persuaded an automobile dealership to provide an additional thousand dollars as a sponsor. I also promised I would be responsible for buying my team's equipment—bats, balls, training tools—and that I would take on the task of find-ing other Senior teams (throughout the metropolitan Phoenix area) to play, as well as schedule games and coordinate umpires for all of our home games (typically, the league would handle most of these responsibilities). Ultimately, I was given a green light from the board of directors.

I started by calling my former Longhorn players, and one by one they enthusiastically agreed to form a Senior team. Some were no longer playing baseball, some were participat-ing in other sports, and some were playing baseball at the high school level. Nevertheless, they all agreed to work out their schedules. Next, I called players on teams we had competed against, and while they didn't personally know me, several of them recalled the Longhorns' 11–0 record. Eventually, I had at least thirteen players who had committed to play. As there were no existing Senior Little League teams in central Phoe-nix, I then contacted the district president to find other Senior Little League teams, throughout metropolitan Phoenix, that would be willing to play us.

The district president had held this position for more than fifteen years and therefore remembered when I had coached previously, in my twenties. Consequently, he went out of his way to help me find teams. Three other teams agreed, two of which were located within fifteen miles of our home field. Our board members continued with their uncertainty.

"Parents of your players will not be involved and won't drive their kids to your games, and none of your sixteen-year-olds have vehicles," they said. "You'll never get your players to show up for away games."

"I'll figure it out," I responded, although I wasn't quite sure what my solution would be. But it was once again the $70-per-day, fifteen-passenger van that I had utilized the previous year. I would drive and tote our team to our away games and back. While it was not the most economical decision, it was a solution nonetheless.

We called our team the Hurricanes, basically as a tribute to Bill, my assistant coach, who was undergoing surgery at the time. Bill was a graduate of the University of Miami—the Hurricanes. Jonathan would attend every practice and would be late for only one game the entire season; he showed up during the second inning of that one because of a meeting with his parole officer. He apologized and explained profusely as he scrambled to put on his uniform. It was one of the few times I would look over and view Jonathan sitting on the bench; he would play the last two innings of that game and help us to secure an 8–0 win. Throughout the season, Jonathan spent a lot of time at our house; he went swimming with us, went to a hotel for a weekend with my family, and spent the Fourth of July with us, eating pizza and watching fireworks from the roof of our house.

He invited me to "kick-back" parties and tried to persuade me to have one at our house. I'm not sure I ever fully understood what took place at these "kick-back" parties, but I assumed there were a lot of drinking and recreational activities going on. His mind was spinning as he explained to me how we would make hundreds of dollars, thanks to the size of our house and based on an entrance fee of five to ten dollars per person. Jonathan described how bouncers would handle weapon control by frisking every person entering the party. I told him I didn't think our neighbors would appreciate this type of party. Apparently, some "kick-back" parties allowed weapons and others didn't. We never had the party, and I never attended one.

Coaching the Hurricanes did not keep me from spending time with my family. During the summer of 2007 we traveled to Chicago. We visited famous Wrigley Field, toured Northwestern University, took a boat tour along the Chicago River, and ate deep-dish pizza. Upon arriving at Wrigley Field, we discovered that our tickets were for bleacher seats, which wasn't a problem until we realized that bleacher seats meant general-admission seating. We had arrived too late to find five seats together.

All five of us found an open spot to stand with our backs up against the railing. It wasn't ideal, but we were at least standing in world-famous Wrigley Field. Plus, we had a clear view of the field and figured we could eat a "dog," stay four or five innings, and head out with a good enough experience.

This plan worked until a younger guy, probably in his twenties, and his girlfriend squeezed into a spot next to us; no problem, except room was sparse, and essentially this guy was standing directly in front of Briana.

"Hey, could you move over?" I asked. "There's not enough room for you two to stand here. You are blocking my daughter's view of the game."

This guy was bigger than me, younger than me, and a little rough around the edges; moreover, he didn't like my request. He said, "That's the way it is out here, buddy."

"I'm not your buddy, and maybe you just need to move along," I said.

He didn't move along, and it didn't help matters that he and his girlfriend were smoking, which obviously is not allowed anywhere in the ballpark. Finally an usher came over and told them, "No smoking in the ballpark."

"Says who?" the guy snarled, taking a puff and blowing smoke at the usher's face. Whereupon I, of course, felt the need to intervene in support of the usher.

"Hey, I believe smoking is prohibited at every ballpark in the country," I said.

By now Briana was looking up at me as if to say, "Dad, that's enough." Her eyes got even a little bigger when I shot back at the intruder, "Why don't you take your smoking outside the stadium so my daughter can see the game!"

That seemed to shut the guy up, and eventually, the couple wandered off. Maybe I shouldn't have returned fire, but that's just not my style. I never truly understood why he just didn't kick my ass; he certainly could have. In any event, it gave me another juicy story with which to regale Lyn later, as we all rode the "L" back to our hotel. She'd been nearby but wasn't completely aware of what was happening and hadn't heard the entire conversation. I knew that the Hurricanes would also get a kick out of their coach's big baseball confrontation.

At the Cubs' game; one small (soon to be filled) standing spot next to Briana

Chapter 26

Rolling with the Hurricanes

THE HURRICANES PERFORMED MUCH BETTER than I had ever expected. With each game, we improved our individual skills as we learned how to play the game the right way. This meant a lot more than just winning.

In one game, we were absolutely crushing a team, by about ten runs after only two innings. One by one our players would step up to the plate and drive the ball somewhere in the out-field. As the opposing team replaced pitcher after pitcher to find some relief, I approached my entire team and insisted that no bases would be stolen through the remainder of the game.

"This team is struggling, and there's no reason to rub it in their face," I said. "Play hard and take your cuts at the plate; however, no stealing until I say otherwise."

In the third inning we had increased our lead to 15–0, and

the umpires were simply waiting for four and a half innings to be completed so they could officially end the game via the ten-run rule. E-man had just driven a single into right-center field and was standing on first base. When the ball dribbled away from the catcher on the next pitch, he decided he was going to steal second base. The catcher's throw to second was late, and E-man was safe. I raised my hands high, indicating a time-out to the umpire. I walked out to second base and quietly told E-man that he was out of the game because he failed to follow my instructions. He didn't argue but walked off the field with attitude. I put in a substitute runner, and as I walked back to my coaching box, I apologized to the opposing coach. He nodded his understanding.

Our team developed many traditions, not only to avoid the mundane, but also to help maintain order, structure, and consistency. After every game, we would walk into the outfield and every player would take a seat for a postgame talk. Parents were not allowed to be within hearing distance. In these talks, we spoke of the game, discussing both positive and negative aspects, including exceptional plays by particular players. Also, I would award offensive and defensive players of the game. Although we would sometimes get carried away with joking and celebrating during these talks, everyone would quiet down when I announced the players of the game—each one was awarded a five-dollar gift card to Foot Locker or Big 5 Sporting Goods. Throughout the season, particular players would accumulate a handful of gift cards, enabling them to total anywhere from twenty-five to fifty dollars in store credits. The cost of these cards came out of my pocket but was well worth it, as the cards assigned credibility to the selection process.

Another tradition involved preseason and postseason parties. At the beginning of every season I would host a party following a Friday afternoon practice. New players were often hesitant, thinking that a party at a middle-age coach's house would obviously be boring and ultimately a waste of a Friday night. However, returning players would advise them otherwise. We cooked hot dogs and hamburgers and ordered pizza. Our daughters always attended the parties and often would invite their girlfriends, which was popular among the players. We swam, played basketball, competed in PlayStation games, and traditionally had a foosball tournament. Players were randomly paired up by drawing names out of a hat; as a result, two players who rarely spoke to each other might find themselves on the same side of the foosball table in a competitive doubles match. After most teams were eliminated, the winning team and the second-place team would receive awards ranging from gift cards to headphones. These parties often helped cure preseason conflicts that always existed between players; by the time our first regular-season game arrived, the party had resulted in memories that would help the players bond.

Postseason parties also took place at my house, and let's just say a season of bonding had taken place among the players by then. There was no need to pair up players, and few player conflicts remained. At one particular party our daughters and their girlfriends, one by one, were tossed over a player's shoulder and into the pool. I too found myself at the bottom of the pool; however, it took at least three players to get me there. Lyn was spared.

Throughout the season, Angel struggled to perform. Although he was one of our better players and had been a part of the undefeated Longhorn team the previous year, Angel's attendance was inconsistent throughout the 2007 season. Just one week before our first all-star game, Angel quit the team, opting to work hours that sometimes extended into the night. His parents' residence reportedly housed seven or eight people, including brothers, sisters, and cousins. According to Angel, he needed to work to help support the family. We never questioned his decision, and we made it clear that he was welcome to return to the team at any time. And so he did. Yet, because of his late return and corresponding lack of attendance at practices, I limited his playing time. While other players questioned my decision to bench one of our star players, Angel understood and quietly sat in the dugout until his time came to enter the game.

Angel was never without a girlfriend—I should say girlfriends. Although only about five feet five inches tall, Angel was dark-skinned and charming. On occasion during practice, I would see him leaning against the outfield fence, luring any teenage girl who happened to be passing by. Because he was Angel, they would stop and chat; I would have to yell at him to get back on the field. His demeanor ranged from quiet and removed to high-strung; at several practices players would joke by making references to "la coca," implying that he *had* to be on cocaine. He would challenge hitters in batting practice and sprint and dive all over the field, attempting to catch or stop (even with his diving body) every ball that was hit. During our van trips, every time the song *Beautiful Girl* by Sean Kingston would play on the radio (and somehow it was *always* on the radio), Angel would proudly and loudly sing along.

On other occasions he would quit during practice, sitting in the dugout and refusing to participate in drills. "Angel, get up!" Emmanuel would yell. E-man had grown up, played ball, and gone to school with Angel. "Angel, you're an ass!" continued E-man.

"Shut the fuck up," answered Angel. "You're a suck-up to Coach."

"Oh, hell no," stammered E-man. "I just wanna play . . . I'm fired up . . . we're gonna kick some ass in all-stars. Get your ass out here."

Angel remained in the dugout, regardless of E-man's coaxing and my warning that if he did not participate in practice drills, he would not play in all-stars. I wasn't quite sure what provoked his attitude. When I asked, he always responded, "Coach, it's not baseball or you."

For the majority of the year, Preston performed as our cleanup hitter. Although this was the only year I coached Preston, he had become a leader on the team, as well as a close friend of mine and my family. In previous years, Preston always had been the first player picked in Little League, and as I never seemed to draw the first draft pick, he had always played on opposing teams. However, because our 2007 team was the only Senior team, I finally had the opportunity to coach Preston, after coaxing him to play. At about six feet two inches, he was thin and athletic.

Preston had missed all of our preseason practices, as he was competing in the state championship with the varsity tennis team at his high school. That, coupled with his status as a new-comer and somewhat of an outsider, meant that Preston had to work to fit into the chemistry of the team. Out of fairness to all of the players who had struggled through a month of pre-season practices, Preston played only a few innings per game during the first three games of the season. He never com-plained about his lack of playing time, and as the season pro-gressed, he would prove his leadership and his athletic ability. In a subsequent year, Preston would tell me his first thought had been to decline to play Senior-league baseball, as he was already committed to tennis and was working part-time during the summer as an archaeological intern. However, he decided to play for our team and juggle all three activities. He said he was inspired by my "history of coaching" and the time I had been willing to devote to coaching while operating a business and suffering from a brain tumor.

Early in the regular season, in order to celebrate a particu-larly impressive win on the road, I decided to stop the van at a Circle K convenience store and allow every player to get one snack and one beverage. After our next win, as we pulled away from the opposing team's field, players started chanting, "Cir-cle K, Circle K, Circle K." This thirty- to forty-dollar pit stop became a tradition for every away game thereafter. Even with-out any monitoring, no player would ever attempt to buy more than two items. However, as they passed through the checkout line, single file, without exception E-man would be the last in line. And, on more than one occasion, he would show up with a six-pack of beer or a box of condoms, just to make sure I, or the cashier, was paying attention. This tradition continued for two years, including the district championship and state tournament. A handful of Circle K attendants actually got to know our players, as we frequented their store on a regular basis.

At least once during every practice I would walk around, monitoring the drills the players were working on. "It's all about the journey . . . it's all about the journey," I would always remind them. Their initial response was, "Coach, what the hell does that mean?" I explained that we were on a journey to the state tournament. I had no idea when I said it whether we would even qualify to compete as an all-star team, nor did I know if we could earn our way to the tournament. Nevertheless, I would repeat this phrase over and over, practice after practice. And if I failed to recite the phrase on any given day, they would remind me: "Coach, it's all about the journey, right? We're on a journey, right, Coach?" It became a motto in which they believed.

In our final three games of the 2007 season, we finished strong. I was continuously thinking about all-stars but wasn't sure if our team would qualify. After all, an all-star team comprised the best players among a number of teams. We were just a team. As a result, as the season came to an end, I wasn't sure if I was experiencing the last few games in which I would have the privilege of coaching these kids.

I had coached many of these players for the past few years; I had become a part of their lives, and they a part of mine. Competing in a postseason tournament would be reflective of our trials and tribulations as a team. Luckily, we got the chance to play.

Chapter 27

The Chance of a Lifetime

AFTER WINNING THE DISTRICT CHAMPIONSHIP, a best-of-three series against a north Phoenix all-star team that comprised players selected from two regular-season teams, we traveled to Bullhead City to compete in the state tournament. We were one of only eleven district champions in the entire state of Arizona.

"Good luck!"

"You're out of your mind!"

"What are you thinking?"

I heard all of these responses when I told people I was taking a group of fourteen- to sixteen-year-old boys from the inner city on a weeklong trip to play baseball, with only my wife as additional adult supervision, at least on the bus and in the hotel where we would be staying. I attributed these reactions to a lack of faith, or shortsightedness; these people were obviously incapable of understanding my motivation. Did they have no sense of pursuing a challenge in life, regardless of the obstacles? What could possibly happen?

When I approached our league about continuing on to the state tournament, the board of directors indicated that funds were limited. Further, as they had previously warned me, they were concerned about the lack of adult supervision on the trip, as few parents would make the journey to Bullhead City. Nevertheless, the league provided two thousand dollars toward the trip; expenses beyond this amount were my responsibility or the responsibility of players' parents. Because most boys had limited funds from their families, Lyn and I personally paid for all additional expenses (nearly $4,500). On top of that amount, I handed out fifty dollars to each player during the initial bus ride; I told them they could spend it as they pleased during the trip. A few would actually purchase baseball bats, batting gloves, or even sweatbands from a local sporting-goods store. Despite costs that far exceeded the funds provided by the league, it was worth it: the experience for these boys was something they will remember for the remainder of their lives.

Two moms made the trip, but they traveled separate from the team. I rented a bus with a personal driver named Joe, and we headed for Bullhead City, with all the players, Lyn, Briana, and Olivia. Only one of my two assistant coaches could attend the games during the weeklong trip. However, he was unable to travel with the team and he could not stay at the hotel before and after the games. Rather, Bill would work a half-day in Phoenix and drive all afternoon (it was about a five-hour trip) to arrive for a 5:00 or 6:00 p.m. game. After the game, he would drive through the night back to Phoenix and reliably be at work at 8:00 the next morning. This act, in itself, provides a perfect example of Bill's character; every day, throughout the week of the state tournament, I could count on Bill arriving on time for our game.

The "stage" for state baseball tournaments should be college stadiums, minor-league ballparks, or spring-training facilities. After all, each of these types of facilities exists right in our backyard in Phoenix. However, on the opening day of the tournament, it was 110 degrees on a dusty baseball field in Bullhead City, Arizona, in the middle of the Mojave Desert. As far as we were concerned, it was the middle of nowhere. The facility, a twenty-five-minute drive from our hotel in Laughlin—actually part hotel, part casino—contained a half-broken scoreboard, one of those old scoreboards where an eight looks like a three, thanks to several broken or burnt-out lightbulbs. Further, umpires had to explain the ground rules regarding holes in the fence: "If the ball rolls through one of the holes in the outfield fence, tell your players to raise their hands." I suppose there were so many holes, no one thought repairing them was a very good idea.

During one of our games the sprinklers popped up and started soaking our players. During another game one of the umpires was throwing Skittles at my first baseman. Last but not least, because of the extreme heat, no games started before 5:00 p.m. Did anyone consider a different city!?

The tournament was double elimination; two losses and the team was out. Despite our lack of fans, at every game we would step off the bus with confidence, and everyone in Bull-head City knew who our team was and where we were from. Yet no one knew how far these boys had come. I suppose my purpose for the bus, the bus driver, the uniforms, and the rest was to provide a mask of confidence for these boys, if only for one week. Not only had we earned our spot in this tournament, but also we looked good upon arrival.

The majority of our Senior Little League all-star team, if you could call us an all-star team, comprised players whom I had coached for the past two seasons. The teams we were fac-ing were *true* all-star teams, with the best players from multiple teams within a league. We had no league and no other teams to select from. Our team was composed of our regular-season team, as we represented the only Senior team in the Clarendon league.

We won our first game in the state tournament thanks to a technical protest whereby the opposing team was forced to forfeit the game even though they were beating us 7–3 in the sixth inning. Their starting pitcher had thrown more pitches than allowed (Little League regulates the number of pitches a player may throw to protect kids from injuries and to pre-vent coaches from jeopardizing the integrity of a young play-er's pitching arm). After the pitcher had surpassed ninety-five pitches, I told the umpire he had exceeded the legal limit; oddly, the Bullhead City scorekeepers obviously were not monitoring this situation. I suppose this should not have been a surprise to me. There was a long delay while telephone calls were placed to national Little League officials.

Finally, we were awarded the win by forfeit. We received

a lot of glares from the opposing players as we walked over to shake their hands; we were, in fact, a much smaller-sized and far less experienced team. I wasn't sure how my players would react. Would they be disappointed in me for ending the game that way, and would they be embarrassed by winning thanks to a protest? Although we didn't celebrate on the field, to avoid further irritating the much larger opposing players, the feeling on the bus back to the hotel was one of happiness. We had a win in the state tournament, regardless of how it happened.

During the tournament, we were known for our uniforms and our bus. We were also known for Joe, our bus driver, who stood about 5 feet 10 inches, had glasses and thinning hair, and weighed at least 270 pounds. As part of the weeklong rental of the bus, we also got Joe and were required to pay for his hotel room. Joe would not only drive us back and forth to our games, but also randomly join us in other activities, such as meals or a movie. On occasion we would invite him, which seemed like the courteous thing to do. However, Joe then took it upon himself to drive a few of the boys around town, on the bus, to a sporting-goods store or elsewhere, without informing me. I let him know that I was personally responsible for these boys, including knowing where they were at all times.

He would also show up at my room every morning, wanting to know what *we* had planned for the day. He was intruding not only on me but on my family—Briana and Olivia were staying with Lyn and me. Joe would barrel into the room, have a seat on one of the beds, and get comfortable, ready to wait for us to get dressed so he could find out what the plan was for the day.

"Joe, we'll let you know when we need you to drive us to the game; however, as for the rest of the day, and any day, you're free to plan your time *by yourself*," I said. He didn't get the message.

Having traveled across the state of Arizona, with limited facilities available within the hotels and motels that housed the eleven teams competing in the state tournament, teams would show up for their second, third, and fourth games—many of which took place on consecutive days—in dirty uniforms. However, our team needed every possible edge, whether physical or mental. Early in the season I had chosen to reach into my wallet to upgrade our uniforms, and before all-stars, we again upgraded the uniforms by placing player names on the back of each jersey. We were the only team in the tournament with names on our jerseys. Further, with our bright and unique colors and our custom caps, we looked like a class act.

Every night, after each game, all players would drop off their dirt-ground, grass-stained uniforms at my hotel room. It gave me a chance to visit with each player, postgame, on an individual basis. Lyn, Briana, and Olivia would sort and label every uniform—jerseys, pants, and socks—by player name. Then, like clockwork the next morning, they would tote bags of dirty uniforms across the street to a small public laundromat they had discovered.

Two washers and two dryers were housed in a shack of a building, which, of course, was not air-conditioned. It took nearly two hours every morning for them to wash and dry all thirteen uniforms, which they managed by taking shifts. As it was headed for 110 degrees outside, it must have been

120 degrees in the laundromat. I went once to help out and returned to the hotel soaking with sweat. They would sit outside, in the shade, reading books, staying close enough to monitor the machines. On one occasion one of the washers overflowed, spewing water and suds all over the floor. That added an extra hour to their uniform-washing session. But as a result of their efforts, every game, every day throughout the week, our players proudly donned their sparkling-clean uniforms. We looked good.

Chapter 28

Playing for Keeps

BECAUSE OF HIS POOR ATTENDANCE RECORD, Angel did not start the first two all-star games in the state tournament. As a substitute, he had only three at bats in those two games. Did Angel's lack of playing time make a difference in the outcomes? Very possibly, as we trailed in the first game until winning by forfeit and we lost the second game 15–13. Yet the players understood and respected my position. Although we would lose that second game with Angel and E-man sitting on the bench, our team had rallied to lose by only two runs.

To do so we had scored six runs in the final two innings, making the final score respectable and giving our players a little confidence that we could compete at this level. Before our rally, I had spoken to them between innings about continuing to play for pride and respect. I attempted to convince them that we deserved to be at this tournament. They had been lamenting: "Coach, we only won our first game by protest and now we're getting our asses kicked!" They were giving up, and it showed in their performances.

I benched E-man, our starting catcher (and possibly the most talented sixteen-year-old catcher I had ever witnessed), for the final four innings; his actions on the field showed that he had completely given up when we were losing 13–7. Bill and I would not let our players quit. We talked about everything we had gone through as a team to get to this tournament. We reminded them of our two wins over a true all-star team in the district championship. And we encouraged them to keep playing, even harder. Our rally in the last two innings had an impact. On the bus ride back to the hotel, Jonathan said to me, "Coach, we could have beaten that team."

Because our games were never earlier than 5:00 p.m., the boys were essentially free to stay up all night in their rooms, as long as they promised to stay in their rooms, keep quiet, and catch up on their sleep the following day. We usually rounded up everyone (or at least those who actually had slept overnight) sometime between 9:00 and 11:00 a.m., went for breakfast, and spent the day doing a fun activity such as a movie or bowling. We scheduled indoor activities not only to keep the players busy and out of trouble, but also to keep them out of the blistering heat.

Late in the evenings, many players chose to come to my family's room. These late-night gatherings brought about numerous intriguing conversations about sex, drugs, and relationships.

Late night in the hotel room (Adam, Nikk, Preston, Austen, Alex, & Jonathan)

Disappointed by his performance in our loss in the second game of the state tournament, E-man was determined to "leave it all on the field" in the third game. In his mind, doing so started with a good night's sleep. Having stayed up late on previous nights, E-man decided his answer was sleeping pills. He had bought a box of sleeping pills from the hotel store, and he took some—we would never know the exact number—around 10:00 p.m. the day of our second game.

About 2:00 a.m., E-man bolted into our room. He stood at the door, glaring into space, with a wry smile on his face and pupils the size of marbles. The room burst into laughter at the site of E-man, who could do nothing but giggle, stare, and giggle, remaining in this "zombie" state. Other players told us he had taken sleeping pills. Although we were worried about his condition, we felt the best we could do for him was to guide him back to his room and let him sleep.

Our late-night devotees eventually dispersed, but at 4:00 a.m., I received a phone call from Adam, who was one of E-man's roommates. Extremely concerned, Adam said, "I'm in Angel's room calling you. E-man left our room and is wandering through the hallways. When we ran out to get him, we locked ourselves out of our room."

I headed into the hallway and collected E-man, who was trying to get on the elevator. He smiled and said something about needing to get to the game, but he was making little sense. I took him back to Adam and Jonathan and told them to keep him in the hallway while I went downstairs to get a replacement key for their room. When I got back upstairs, E-man was face down in the hallway, sleeping. This was a good thing!

The three of us picked him up, took him to their room, and put him back in bed. We could only hope he would remain passed out. Adam and Jonathan made sure the deadbolt on the door was in place after I left, hoping it would deter the wandering, zombie E-man.

The next morning, E-man couldn't remember anything about the overnight incidents; in fact, he truly believed we were all making up the entire story. But the rest of us would never forget his bulging eyes, his giggle, and his wide smile when he walked into our room.

Another late night meet-up resulted in confessions among the players, almost as though they wanted to come clean with me. Whether we wanted to know or not, we found out who were virgins and who weren't. I'm not sure who I believed and who I didn't. We also learned more concerning their relationships with their parents. And without being provoked, Jonathan confessed to all of us that he had been selling drugs and guns for the previous two years.

As the week went along, I got to know more about Jonathan. He had been a member of a gang. When a fight had broken out at Jonathan's high school in a previous year, security cameras at the school identified him as the "crew" leader, and he was suspended from school. A crew, though not a gang, is a group of guys who hang together and fight together; all crews have a leader. As part of Jonathan's suspension, he was forbidden from setting foot on the school campus. When a security guard spotted Jonathan on campus, he was arrested and expelled from school. He had continued to take high school classes via an online program.

Jonathan had an uncle who went to prison for fifteen years and a friend whose body was found chopped into pieces in the trunk of a car in Mexico following an attempt to buy drugs. When Jonathan was seventeen, after our Longhorns season and before the Hurricanes season, he was a member of a gang and was busted for possession of a "dirty"—stolen—weapon. Driving with a "homie," a friend and gang leader, in a car filled with drugs and weapons, he soon found himself jumping out of a moving vehicle and running for his life from police who had attempted to pull the car over for a minor traffic violation. His homie recently had been released from prison after doing time for armed robbery, and he and Jonathan had become partners in dealing drugs and weapons. So Jonathan ran.

Although Jonathan was caught, his homie, who owned the car, was the one charged with possession of drugs and illegal weapons. Jonathan could be charged only with resisting arrest, with no connection to the weapons and guns in the car. However, his friend, in an effort to reduce the charges he faced, claimed that Jonathan owned one of the dirty weapons. As a result, Jonathan was arrested and spent days in a juvenile facility. For the next three years he fought the charge; had he been found guilty, he would have faced five to ten years in prison. He served probation, was subjected to random drug tests, and ultimately left the gang.

To join a gang, one had to be "jumped" in, and to leave one had to be "jumped" out. Being jumped amounted to a random beating by the largest guys in the gang. It was meant to ensure the loyalty of the member being jumped in or out—that the member would not betray the gang. Jonathan was allowed to leave the gang without being jumped out. However, his court date would be extended month after month, year after year, until final sentencing took place in 2010. He will always recall that our 2007 baseball team kept him off the streets, kept him out of trouble, and ultimately encouraged him to leave the gang during our 2007 season.

He apologized to all of us in the room, as many of these incidents took place during the Longhorns season and a portion of the Hurricanes season. But most important, he vowed to me at that moment never to deal drugs or guns again. One year later, as I sat in chemotherapy, I received a text from Jonathan: "Watz sup coach? How u n ur wife doin? Juz to let ya kno, stayin outa trouble . . . no drugs." I believed him.

Although that season would turn out to be the end of my Little League coaching career, it would also prove to be a springboard for a continuing relationship with a group of guys who were more than just a baseball team. Through our successes and failures and medical conditions, they had learned from me and I had learned from them, and the relationship would continue well beyond our last game.

Chapter 29
The Final Out

IN JULY 2007, AFTER A SUCCESSFUL regular season, an all-star district championship, and two games in the state tournament, these players stood as a team, taking pregame warm-ups in preparation for the most important game of their baseball career: our third game in the tournament.

I had been the leadoff hitter on a high school baseball team that won the Texas state high school championship in 1980—two players from that team would eventually advance to have lucrative careers as professional ballplayers. Even so, at age forty-five I was about to coach what would surprisingly end up being *my* most memorable baseball game as either a player or a coach, and the culmination of an eventful two- to three-year period.

While our record stood at 1–1, we had yet to win a game outright on the field. Notably, no team from the Clarendon league, from any level (Minor, Major, Junior, or Senior), had even advanced to a state tournament since the early 1990s— about fifteen years. Just playing our third game in the state tournament was a huge accomplishment. We easily could have been satisfied with the district championship, for which we received a three-by-six-foot banner to proudly display at our home field in Phoenix. Yet, standing in our hunter-green-and-orange Hurricanes uniforms, with our names or nicknames proudly displayed on the back, we yearned for more than our one win. We wanted a "true" win.

Our two "ace" pitchers, Jonathan and Alvaro, were ineligible to pitch in this third game, as each had reached his pitch-count limit in one of the first two games. The most logical pitcher for this game was Angel, our number three pitcher. Yet on this particular day, Angel's roller-coaster emotions left him unwilling to pitch mentally, and therefore physically. I turned away from Angel, disappointed, and looked at Preston. "Coach, I'll pitch," he responded before I could even ask.

In the bottom of the first inning, as he commenced the most important game of his pitching career, Preston faced only three hitters. He started out somewhat shaky as he walked the first one; they had a runner on first base with no outs. The second hitter flied out to left field, and the runner was held at first. The third batter in the lineup drove a hard line drive to the outfield, where Freddy, our right fielder, sprinted in to attempt a play. Although Freddy possessed incredible speed, he had been known to occasionally misjudge a few fly balls in the outfield. As a result, I stopped breathing for a few seconds— any misjudgment by Freddy would result in the ball rolling all the way to the outfield fence, scoring the runner from first base and likely rewarding the hitter with a triple. However, not only did Freddy and the ball meet each other in the middle of right field, resulting in an incredible and surprising running catch, but Freddy also fired the ball to first base to double off the runner, who stood, more stunned than I, somewhere between first and second base. The first inning was over . . . we had a 2–0 lead.

In the top of the second inning we made it 3–0 with a walk and stolen base from Adam and an RBI single by Freddy.

By the bottom of the fifth inning, Jonathan's arm was so sore—he had pitched a complete seven-inning game the previous day—that his hand was shaking. However, his commitment and competitiveness would not allow him to tell me; it was only after other players informed me of his condition that I approached him on the field. He argued to stay in the game, but we needed him to rest his arm in case we needed him to pitch in the next game. Disappointed, Jonathan strolled off the field. Alvaro took his place, in spite of our desperate need for Jonathan's defense at shortstop.

Our opponent, East Mesa, sent eight players to the plate and scored three runs that inning to take a 5–4 lead. Preston had two balks and four wild pitches in the inning, but he had an incredible pitching performance through four and two-thirds innings before I replaced him with Angel. Preston had given up only one earned run and five hits, had thrown eighty-four pitches, and had kept us in the ballgame. His performance may have motivated Angel to agree to pitch.

Alvaro, our third hitter in the top of the sixth inning, drew a walk and scored a run to tie the game at 5. Although Alvaro didn't play on our Longhorns team, I had coached him two years earlier in the Junior division. His family, from Mexico, spoke broken English, and he lived in a mobile home park about two miles from the Clarendon baseball field—too far to walk. His sponsor, or "big brother," was an elderly man named Leon. Leon signed him up for baseball, every season, and often would drive Alvaro to and from practice. For some of the regular-season practices and most games, I would swing by Alvaro's house to pick him up and, afterward, drop him off. If one or both of my daughters were driving home with us, as happened on several occasions, Alvaro would tell me he had moved to a nearby apartment complex and we should just drop him off there. I realized quickly that he was somewhat embarrassed, in front of my daughters, of his mobile home residence. On the first occasion, my daughter Briana asked, "He still lives at the mobile home park, doesn't he?" I nodded, and she understood.

Later in the sixth inning, two singles, one by Preston and one by Alan, scored the go-ahead run and gave us a 6–5 lead. As our team stormed the field in the bottom of the inning with its one-run lead, Jonathan met me on the field with one request: "Coach, you have to put me back in."

"Jon, your arm is shot . . . if you tear something, you're done for the rest of the tournament," I replied. No response. As a coach, I shouldn't have let him return to the game and risk injury. Yet as a competitor, I understood his desire. "OK, take shortstop . . . let Alvaro know." And he headed to his position.

Although East Mesa scored one run to once again tie the game, Jonathan made two incredible plays at shortstop, including diving for a line drive that would have extended the inning, had it gotten past him. As he jogged off the field, his smile spread across his entire face. I'm not sure if it was a thank-you for allowing him to return to the game or a form of "I told you so!"

At the end of seven innings the game remained tied, so we forged ahead into extra innings. In the top of the eighth, our first batter walked, stole second base, and advanced to third on a wild pitch. Our second hitter was Jonathan. The call seemed obvious. I carried out a series of signals, ending with a right hand to the ear and then below the waist. Both the runner on third and Jonathan responded by tipping their helmets. The suicide squeeze was on.

A suicide squeeze entails the runner on third bolting for home as soon as the pitcher commits to pitch to the hitter; at this point the hitter has no choice but to bunt the ball, anywhere, anyhow, just as long as he puts the ball on the grass. If he succeeds, the runner scores; if he misses the ball, the runner is a dead duck. Jonathan squared around to bunt and, in spite of the ball being thrown directly toward his head, dropped the baseball right on the grass. As a result, the pitcher and catcher had no time to react, and the run scored. We led the game 7–6.

In the bottom of the eighth inning the opposing team failed to score, and this group of inner-city boys had won their second game of the state tournament, this time with an impressive victory over a much more talented and experienced team. It was 11:30 p.m.—the game had lasted more than four hours. Our players stormed the field, piling on top of each other, throwing their hats and gloves in the air, and celebrating as though we had just won the Little League World Series. In many ways we had. During the process, two of our players successfully dumped a cooler of Gatorade over my head . . . I was now an official coach.

We lost our next game, a competitive match, 6–2 to finish the state tournament with two wins and two losses. The top four teams advanced to the state "playoffs," and we and one other team had identical records—we were tied for fourth place. Nevertheless, we were edged out based on average runs allowed per inning during the four games. Our team allowed an average of 0.9 runs per inning, while the team with which we were tied had allowed 0.7 runs per inning.

However, our team had accomplished what no other Clarendon team had achieved in fifteen years: a trip to the state tournament. And they had accomplished even more: two respectable wins and a tie for fourth place among ten highly competitive and more experienced teams.

Adam, Jay, Jonathan and Preston (Olivia in background) at the bowling alley

To celebrate our appearance in the state tournament, I reserved a suite for an Arizona Diamondbacks game. Costly, yes, but the large majority of our players had not, and might never again, see the inside of a private suite at any type of professional sporting event. The day of the game, Alan called and asked Lyn if he was supposed to wear a suit to the game— a naive, yet very sincere and humble question. Lyn told him jeans or shorts would be just fine.

All players were to meet at our baseball field beforehand so we could travel as a team. The plan was for a Hummer limo to arrive at our house so we could surprise the guys as we approached the baseball field. We had contracted with the same company that had provided the bus to the state tournament, and we had requested not to have Joe as a driver, since the relationship had become a little strange in Bullhead City and we had only enough suite tickets for our family and the players.

The doorbell rang, I opened the door, and there stood Joe. "Are the guys here yet?" he asked.

I was stunned—more so when I looked out to the driveway and saw a bus, not a Hummer limo.

I asked, "Where the hell is the Hummer?"

"Oh, sorry about that," Joe said. "A Hummer wasn't available."

Lyn and I spent fifteen minutes on the phone with the transportation company, irately inquiring as to what had happened. They promised that a Hummer limo would be available to pick us up after the game, and with few alternatives, we proceeded with Joe to pick up our players. Because they never knew about the Hummer, all of the players were excited about the game as we pulled up in the bus.

The suite was catered with food and drinks, which the players devoured. Between innings I awarded plaques and trophies for offensive player of the year, defensive player of the year, and most valuable player. Jonathan received the latter. After the game Bill, who was employed by the Phoenix Suns, took us over to US Airways Center, where our players were given a private tour, including the inside of the locker rooms and the private practice court in the basement. Again, possibly a once in a lifetime opportunity.

While I remain extremely proud of this team and its accomplishments, I often wonder if I, and these achievements, had much of an impact on their lives. Hollywood's inspirational movies, most of which are based on true stories, end with students or players so inspired by a coach or teacher that their lives are changed, their attitudes are altered, and/or they are inspired to attend college, get jobs, or start families, for example. I can only hope that at least one of my players experienced a life-changing moment or was moved by the success of our team to achieve at a higher level throughout the remainder of his life. I suppose that only time will tell.

Chapter 30

When Man Plans, God Laughs

IN THE FALL, LYN AND I HOSTED AN ANNUAL Halloween party at our house, and 2007 was no exception. The party was for adults; we required everyone to dress up, and we awarded prizes for best male, best female, and best couple costumes. We also incorporated a game every year, including a horror-movie trivia game whereby couples were eliminated one by one when they answered incorrectly, and a *Name That Tune* type of game, where couples would guess Halloween or horror songs based on the first ten notes. Coupled with alcohol, these games were very entertaining.

Lyn and I always dressed as a couple, and our costumes included Dr. Jekyll and Mr. Hyde, the Geico Insurance caveman and gecko, Alfalfa and Darla from *The Little Rascals*, Neo and Trinity from *The Matrix*, and even ladies of the evening.

(I would have struggled to generate even one dollar from any john, but I did have massive boobs and fake eyelashes, and I shaved my legs completely. I was stylin'!)

Lyn and I as "Ladies of the Night" with Briana . . . I'm the one to the left

By the end of 2007, Lefevers Viewpoint Group, Inc. was recognized by the *Phoenix Business Journal* as the second-largest commercial real estate appraisal firm in the metropolitan Phoenix area. We had incredible people, and our gross revenues for the year had hit $2.7 million.

To celebrate, we again went out of town for our holiday party, this time to San Diego, where I rented a small, private yacht for dinner and an evening tour along the coast. We devised another company "game show" activity, modeled after the television hit that had seen me through so many boring nights at the hospital—*Deal or No Deal*.

With me playing the role of Howie Mandel and four spouses volunteering to be the show's models, my employees spent the cruise deciding whether to sell their cases or not. Some won $250. One player won $500. Others didn't do so well. But everyone had fun—even the captain and the crew of the yacht.

My plans for 2008 were to continue to work on regaining and improving my physical strength and condition, to continue the growth of my appraisal company, and to organize a club baseball team, as all of my Longhorns players were now too old to play in Little League, even at the senior level. I was feeling optimistic about my future and confident in my plans. What happened next in my life *might* have been funny . . . if it hadn't been so seriously *not* funny.

Over the course of two years of sitting around in doctors' waiting rooms, undergoing surgeries, taking various medications, and receiving radiation therapy, I'd managed to pack on about fifteen extra pounds. It was time now to take it off. So during the spring of 2008, I started running again. The last time I'd been running had been during the last marathon I'd run, in 2005, while I was in the midst of trying to figure out what was wrong with my foot. I'd slowly redeveloped an ability to walk and jog and run since removal of the tumor, despite having no feeling whatsoever in my right foot and considerable numbness throughout the entire right leg. I'd found out the hard way that I had to be especially cautious of unevenness, dips, plant and tree roots, and holes in any jogging trail I took, because twisting my numb right ankle was a fairly common event.

On many occasions, I would just go down, tumbling to the ground like a two-year-old who can barely walk. I'd trip over the slightest thing—a pebble or any minuscule object on the ground. Though it was funny to see, and sometimes funny to tell someone about, it was also embarrassing.

I figured that to get back fully into running, I just needed to find a running route or path that followed a relatively straight line, with no immediate or sharp turns. I focused on "clean" routes and soon settled into a groove of regular jogging—though admittedly at extremely slow speeds.

Once I had learned to deal with my numb foot, I began to suffer from another physical problem, shortness of breath. I'd never had problems of that nature before, even when I was running for longer distances and at much faster speeds. I couldn't figure out what was going on. For a while I shrugged it off as just a by product of being so out of shape. I figured the breathing problems would go away as my fitness level increased. But they didn't.

In fact, they reached a new height one day in April, when I was out running with Lyn. I was having so much trouble, I simply couldn't continue. I told her to continue on, but I had to stop, and I turned around and walked back to the house.

My body felt as if it weighed about 400 pounds. And I felt like I was fighting, really struggling, just to breathe; I actually felt like I couldn't gulp in enough air. I felt disgusted with myself. How had I gotten so out of shape? Even with all my health challenges, how and why had I allowed myself to deteriorate to this complete lack of physical conditioning?

Over the next month my breathing condition worsened. I not only struggled to catch my breath after walking up a simple flight of stairs, but I also was unable to sleep in a horizontal position. When lying flat on my back, or on my stomach, I felt as though I was being suffocated and struggled for air. Consequently, I propped up a few pillows and slept at about a forty-five-degree angle.

Lyn had researched my symptoms online and was convinced I had walking pneumonia. I disregarded her Internet diagnosis, but eventually, as reluctant as I was at that point to go see yet another doctor, I agreed to visit our family physician in May.

He ordered an x-ray of my chest. When he got the results, he brought me back in to show me the slides. There was a large mass in my chest.

Chapter 31

Back to the Doctor's Office

I FELT EXACTLY LIKE I'D BEEN SUCKER PUNCHED. And if I felt out of breath before, well, seeing that image of something large and unknown sitting in my chest pretty much knocked the wind out of me altogether.

I scheduled an appointment with Dr. Nakaji, the neuro-surgeon who'd removed my brain tumor. We wanted to make sure the tumor cells that had been in my brain hadn't some-how taken root somewhere else in my body. He booked me for an MRI of the brain and reviewed the x-ray. When the brain scan was clean, with no sign of regrowth of the original brain tumor, he scheduled a more extensive computerized tomography (CT) scan of my chest.

When he summoned me to his office to review the results of the CT scan, his comment went straight to the point: "The good news is, your brain scan looks good, and there are no signs of regrowth associated with the tumor. The bad news is, something else is going on in your chest."

In fact, it *was* pretty bad news, but at least I had some relief in finally figuring out why I'd been experiencing so much trouble breathing. Results of the CT scan revealed that the large mass in my chest was pressing dangerously on my lungs and thereby severely reducing my breathing capacity, as well as causing pain by restricting my arteries.

When I told my neurosurgeon I was taking sleeping pills so I could at least get a few hours of rest every night, he told me emphatically that I had to immediately stop taking them, and that I must never lie flat on my back. "If you keep taking those pills," he said, "you may not wake up one morning."

I decided not to tell him about the one night I had been so uncomfortable and so unable to fall asleep that I had taken two sleeping pills, allowing me to pass out . . . while lying flat on my back. I'd woken from that little experiment struggling just to catch a breath, and I'd felt a severe stinging pain in my left arm. As waking up in the morning was definitely my objective when I lay down to go to sleep every night, I knew I'd follow his advice to a T—so there was no sense worrying him with the risks I'd already unknowingly taken and fortunately lived through.

At the time of this initial discussion, he wasn't sure what the mass was but was convinced it had no correlation with the brain tumor he'd removed. Therefore, he referred me to an oncologist and had my records forwarded to that doctor's office.

I soon began to appreciate the relative calmness of the

preoperative procedures associated with the removal of my brain tumor, because once the mass in my chest was observed, my life became a whirlwind . . . no, make that a tornado.

It was June 2008 now, and once the oncologist got a look at the fourteen-centimeter mass in my chest, he recommended that I immediately admit myself to the hospital, via the emergency room, and await a biopsy to determine what the mass consisted of.

The urgency of his words lit a fire under me. I'd seen before what havoc the delay caused by an inattentive doctor could wreak on my health. This guy was telling me to take immediate action, and therefore I didn't waste time.

That same day, I called my staff together for an emergency meeting. It was 2:00 p.m. on a regular "hump day"—a Wednesday. As far as they all knew, I was in full recovery from the brain tumor, showing up for work every day and getting on with my life. Suffice it to say, this new news was a shock to the company.

I told them I was on my way to the hospital emergency room for a condition that had nothing to do with my former brain tumor. At least 75 percent of my employees had sat in the same conference room about three years earlier and had listened to me describe the scenario associated with that little brush with mortality. Now, once again, I was telling them my health was in dire straits, even though I had no real facts yet.

The employees who'd been around for my earlier battle with the brain tumor were a little less rattled this time. The scenario was sort of familiar to them, and they knew me to be a fighter; they felt fairly confident I would be back soon and all would be well. But the new employees probably were thinking that they might have to start looking for a job, with their boss going off to the emergency room and the future unknown.

I again had brief conversations with Al, who'd now been with me about eight years; Tom, now with me for thirteen years; and Jessica, now in her fifth year. I wasn't worried about the company; though I had no idea what lay ahead for me or how long I'd be out of commission, I knew Lefevers Viewpoint was in good hands with all of them. I said good-bye to my staff, got in my truck, and drove home, where Lyn was waiting to drive me to the emergency room.

I also sent an e-mail to all clients of my company, informing them of what was going on with me personally. I again assured them that I would remain involved in the daily operations, that they would not be affected, and that their appraisal needs would continue to be met with the level of timeliness and professionalism they'd come to expect from Lefevers Viewpoint Group. In other words, I wanted them to know once again that it was business as usual—and that they should continue ordering appraisal reports and expecting the reports to be written in a quality manner and delivered on time. I didn't want any pity from them, and I certainly didn't want any "sympathy work," but I did want them to hear what was going on directly from me, again, rather than hear it from loose talk in the town.

Once I felt that I had my business squared away, I was ready to get my health squared away as well.

Chapter 32

ER "Dramedy"

AT THE RIPE OLD AGE OF FORTY-SIX, believe it or not, I'd never actually been to an emergency room, not even during the brain tumor saga. I had always been under the impression that people waiting in the emergency room were actually there because of an emergency—some dire medical condition that required immediate attention. Hence the term "emergency" room, right?

Wrong. So wrong. When Lyn and I walked through the ER doors, no one but no one—and there were plenty of people there—appeared to be suffering from an actual emergency. You can hear everything in the ER waiting area, and many of the people sitting and standing around were there for relatively simple stuff—one woman complained of having a cold; another had an earache; a man had a cut that wasn't even bleeding.

No matter their "problems," they all had one thing in common, it seemed: no health insurance. And without that, of course, they weren't eligible to go to a family or "regular" doctor for nonemergency treatment. As a result, the waiting room was absolutely mobbed with people seeking medical assistance for what were really pretty routine health problems.

Like others, I sat and waited. My oncologist had told me that when I checked in, I should report that I was having trouble breathing and experiencing numbness and pain in one arm. With those symptoms, I would immediately be considered a legitimate "emergency" patient, and he thought I might be able to get in before other patients in the waiting room who weren't in such physical stress. I did as he recommended, stating, "I have trouble breathing; I have a mass in my chest; I have a numb right leg; and I have a metal plate in my head."

That might have been too much information, but I figured that covered just about everything. Sure enough, my name was called in less than half an hour, and I was taken back for an interview and basic tests. After that initial workup, they put me in a very small, open room with only a curtain for privacy. I was told I was being scheduled for a biopsy, to determine the consistency of the mass, and was also waiting for a private room to become available. Unfortunately, and very uncomfortably, that room would not become available until the middle of the next day, so I passed my first night in the chaos and confusion of a large city hospital's emergency area.

And if I thought spending a night in the intensive care unit, as I'd had to do when I had my brain tumor, was interesting, this night in the ER would prove far more entertaining. It convinced me that all those television dramas that made stars of people such as George Clooney by using emergency room situations for their dramatic (and sometimes comedic) story lines were right on the money.

First, there was absolutely no privacy, as the curtain had little to offer. Second, my so-called bed was merely a gurney. And, for the most part, you could hear and see just about everything and everyone who walked through the emergency room.

"Everyone" would include those admitted in the middle of the night for gunshot wounds and knife stabbings, as a well as a very interesting woman who, to say the least, was not very cooperative. As best I could ascertain, she was on a variety of drugs, had no form of identification, and had to be strapped down to a gurney because she had kicked one of the doctors in the balls. Later, this doctor was questioned by a police officer as to whether he wanted to press charges; he responded, "No, just keep her the hell away from me!" Once strapped down, that lady (and I use the term very loosely here) spent the next two to three hours (still in the middle of the night) screaming and calling just about anyone who entered her vision a "fucking asshole" or "fucking bitch."

Because I had to use the restroom—but truthfully, more out of a morbid sense of curiosity—I got up, rolled my pole with tubes and IV bags attached to it, and walked past the area where she was strapped to her gurney. We made just momentary eye contact, but it was enough to set her off. "Get the fuck out of here!" she screamed at me. Well, at least I wasn't an asshole or a bitch. I waved and kept moving toward the restroom. As I walked away, I recalled my annoyed neighbor from my stay in the hospital two years earlier and had to wonder, "Do I attract these people, or what?"

I did manage to get a few hours of sleep, and the next day I did get put in a private room, from which I was later wheeled up to the fourth floor for the biopsy. It took place via a CT scan; a large needle was plunged into my chest to retrieve a portion of the mass. OK, maybe it wasn't "plunged," like in *Pulp Fiction*, but it was rather rapidly inserted. I was awake for the procedure, but happily drugged with gas and numbed up.

By Thursday afternoon I was told that the results likely would not be available until Monday, yet they wanted me to stay in the hospital through the weekend. No way, I thought, and I immediately began to lobby for my oncologist to release me from the hospital so I could go home for the weekend. He strongly recommended against my leaving the hospital; he wanted me to continue to have my vitals monitored, and besides, he said, the results of the tests could become available at any time, hopefully sooner than Monday.

I was skeptical, and I wasn't entirely sure we were communicating well in the first place. My oncologist was originally from Czechoslovakia, had a thick accent, and was sometimes difficult to understand. I expected to struggle to understand the medical lingo, but many times I was left wondering whether he was even speaking English. He was blunt in his speech, but also vague. Blunt I could handle, but vague didn't work so well for me.

About the same time, the radiologist who had administered radiation to me after my brain tumor stopped by my room to visit me. He worked at the hospital, had heard I was admitted, and came by to see what was going on.

After hearing of my dilemma, and after hearing me petition for my release, my radiologist pulled out his cell phone (hey, I thought we weren't supposed to use those in patients' rooms!), called my oncologist, and persuaded him to cut me loose. Now that is customer service! I was released on Friday, and I promised I would readmit myself the following week. I was thrilled to be able to spend that weekend in the comfort of my own bed, although I use the word "comfort" lightly, and in the reassurance of my family.

Throughout the weekend, I experienced sharper pains in my left arm, typically during the middle of the night; sometimes the pain was so intense, I would struggle just to lift my arm. I would later find out the reason: The mass was pressing on the arteries surrounding my heart—which meant that, in addition to the threat of suffocating while sleeping because of the restriction of air flow, my body was now experiencing mild strokes.

On Monday morning, since I hadn't heard anything about the biopsy results over the weekend, I went to my office to do some work. The call came later in the day, and I was told that the biopsy had been unsuccessful in diagnosing the mass. Essentially, the sample taken was too small. I would need to readmit myself, via the wonderful emergency room once again, for a more intrusive biopsy—the equivalent of minor surgery—so that a much larger sample of the mass could be taken. I asked for a couple of days, and on Wednesday afternoon I readmitted myself to the hospital for another biopsy.

On one occasion, during one of the many CT scans I was scheduled for, the technicians were continuously attempting to force me to lie on my back, saying this was the only way they could successfully administer the scan. Over and over, I repeated that when lying on my back, for the most part I could not breathe. Unbelievably, they would suggest to me that I just needed to relax and that it was very common for patients to become stressed and hyperventilate during testing. I was beyond frustrated. Weren't these guys aware of why I was there in the first place?

"Believe me, I've had numerous scans and MRIs, and this has nothing to do with stress," I'd explain each time. "It's because the mass is restricting my breathing." But nobody seemed to be really listening, though they did keep nodding their heads, patronizingly, when I told them these things.

Being forced to lie down in a way that my doctor had warned me could kill me was pretty much the only thing causing me stress. But I decided I'd do what they told me to and let them see what happens.

So, I lay down on the table, flat on my back, and the technicians left the room to initiate the scan. In less than a minute, the two technicians came rushing back into the room, yelling, "Get up! Get up! You're turning blue!"

I scrambled to an upright position, caught my breath, and repeated to them, "Maybe because I can't breathe—like I told you!" Thereafter, they listened to me very carefully and treated me with the utmost attention. But hell, read the charts, guys!

After all the preliminary preparations, I was ready for the second biopsy, which would require minor surgery. I would be put under anesthesia, and an incision would be made in my chest so the doctors could remove a large enough piece of the mass to get relevant biopsy results.

The biopsy was successful, with just two hitches: I apparently had difficulty breathing under an anesthetic, so a breathing tube had to be inserted during the surgery. And, after the surgery, my overall condition and vital signs were less than desirable, so I was placed into intensive care for recovery. It was a familiar place for me.

I remember waking up with a very, very sore throat. It was June 12, my birthday, and Preston—of all people—would be the first person to show up in my room in intensive care. As he stood there with flowers and a dozen chocolate chip cookies (which he actually made), the nurse asked if he was family, as only family members were allowed in the ICU. My response, with IVs and tubes protruding from all over my body, was, "He's my second son . . . he can stay."

I'm not sure the nurse knew what exactly that meant; however, she let him stay.

Meanwhile, Lyn, Briana, Adam, and Olivia were waiting outside my original room, on a different floor. No one had bothered to tell them that because of my problems breathing during surgery and my poor condition, I'd been relocated to the ICU.

When I asked Preston where they were, he told me, "I haven't seen them; I just asked what room you were in at the front desk, and they sent me here." I sent him out to see if he could find them—I knew they probably didn't know where I was—and he ventured out around the hospital and finally found them sitting in a general waiting room . . . waiting.

Preston approached them and calmly said, "Jay's in intensive care, due to complications during the biopsy . . . I just talked to him." Of course my family was caught off guard—they didn't expect to see Preston and certainly didn't expect him to have seen me before they did. And all of them were wondering, "Shouldn't Jay's doctor be telling all this to us?"

Meanwhile, I was having more fun, TV-worthy drama in the ICU than I'd had even in the emergency room. The large ICU room I was placed in was divided by a curtain and intended for two patients. I had the room to myself—until a nurse wheeled my roommate in on a gurney, followed by two police officers. Always a good sign.

Then I noticed that though he was unconscious, my roomie was handcuffed to the gurney. Not necessarily the vision of an ideal roommate. Later, it was explained to us that he was a convict in prison who'd had a heart attack in his jail cell and had just undergone bypass surgery. I was simply happy the guy was quiet and not screaming the F-bomb at everyone who walked by. The two police officers never left his side, and though their charge was unconscious, it didn't bother me a bit to have them there in case he woke up feeling antsy.

As a birthday present to me, the nurse promised me she would get me out of the ICU and into a private room by the end of the day, and she did.

Preston made appearances at the hospital for the next two days, showing up with a birthday present and the board game Yahtzee. He hung around for hours to keep me company while I waited for the material taken from my chest to be biopsied and evaluated. We never got around to playing Yahtzee; however, we vowed we would eventually, someday, "play some dice." (Later that summer, I would periodically receive text messages from Preston, asking how I was doing. He didn't ask whether we would ever form a club baseball team, but he asked just one simple question, "Coach, when are we going to play some dice?" "One of these days," I'd text him back. "One of these days.")

I honestly don't remember if Preston was there when I got the results from my biopsy. I don't remember where I was in the hospital, what time of day it was—I don't even remember who told me. But the diagnosis I remember.

I had cancer. Specifically, non-Hodgkin's lymphoma.

Chapter 33

The "Big C"

FOR THE MOST PART, FROM THE MOMENT the mass in my chest was discovered, it had been indicated to me that cancer was a strong possibility. After all, none of the physicians had any other logical explanation for the mass. Therefore, I can't say that I was necessarily surprised or saddened by the diagnosis of non-Hodgkin's lymphoma. I reacted as per normal for me: I took in the information and focused on figuring out what to do next.

Looking back, I again imagine a scene in a movie where the patient is told that he or she has cancer. It's always an emotional scene, isn't it? The entire family huddles together with the patient to cry or offer consolation on the supposed death sentence that people always seem to think goes hand in hand when the "Big C" is mentioned. Then, of course, the handsome or beautiful doctor tells the family to be strong and encourages them to focus on the positive and start aggressive treatment. "We can beat this thing," they always tell them.

I have no such scene from my own reality. I just remember immediately starting in with my questions: "When will chemo start?" "How many chemo treatments do I need?" "What the hell is non-Hodgkin's?" Answers came—not always the ones I wanted to hear, but at least I had a plan for moving forward. And I had my family, who knew better than to huddle around me, crying. Instead they got busy. When I arrived home from the hospital, I found that, as a belated birthday present, they'd all decided to give me a La-Z-Boy chair, which would enable me to sleep partially upright to alleviate the breathing difficulty and discomfort from that heavy mass bearing down on everything in my chest. It was the perfect gift.

Before I was released, though, I underwent an additional minor surgery for installation of a "port"—or "portacath"—in my chest. The port, which was surgically placed approximately one inch below the skin, would provide access for chemotherapy treatments as the port, via a catheter, was directly connected to a main artery and would receive needles inserted through the skin. Drugs could be injected and blood samples drawn—both of which would happen very frequently during the course of my treatment—with far less discomfort for the patient, aka me.

During the summer of 2008 our family vacation was postponed for obvious reasons. Briana had been accepted into a theater intern program at Northwestern University in Chicago; yet when she heard of my condition, she questioned whether she should attend the five-week program. In addition, Adam was selected as a youth ambassador, a representative from his school who would be an exchange student in one of several participating countries. His selected country was China. Both opportunities were incredible; Briana and Adam had each endured a rigorous selection process. Therefore, I told them that under no circumstances were they to reconsider their trips. Whether they were around or not, I would fight the cancer and beat it, one day at a time. In the meantime, they would experience what could be once in a lifetime opportunities.

Adam left in the first half of June, while Briana headed out for Chicago toward the end of June. Adam spent three weeks in Chengdu, China, living with his partner exchange student's family, then returned with his exchange student for three weeks back in the U.S. When they arrived, we found Leon, the Chinese student, to be intelligent, courteous, and ambitious. We talked politics and culture and did our best to show him what America was all about. We traveled to Chicago to drop off Briana and spent the weekend. Nights were rough, but I always looked forward to mornings, as the daytime activities took my mind away from the physical ramifications from chemotherapy. When we dropped off seventeen-year-old Briana, we cried as we hugged; it took me a while to let go of her. I just kept hugging her.

I was scheduled to begin receiving chemotherapy at the end of June. There were to be up to eight chemo treatments, taking place once every three weeks. If the chemo were successful in diminishing the mass sufficiently, I'd then go on radiation to finish the job and knock the cancer out of my body.

In the weeks before my treatment began, nights in the La-Z-Boy seemed to last forever. I actually dreaded going to sleep every night, waiting for the stinging pain and breathing problems, and I couldn't wait for chemotherapy to commence—if you can imagine such a thing. My oncologist told me the mass should start shrinking after about two chemotherapy treatments, and I was eager to get there.

Months later I would sell the La-Z-Boy chair. Even though it had been a wonderful, very nice leather chair and a much appreciated present from my family, I came to associate it too closely with the countless sleepless nights and consider it too representative of the physical and psychological pain of that period. It served its purpose. Well done, La-Z-Boy. Well done.

Normally, chemo treatments are scheduled to be split over two days, as the process entails several hours of slow, dripping infusions via an intravenous system. But I persuaded the chemotherapy staff and nurses to allow the entire treatment to take place in one day, on Mondays, thereby enabling me to miss only one day of work every three weeks. My plan was chemo on Monday, be back at work on Tuesday.

However, as a result of my decision, that one day comprised seven to eight hours of sitting in a recliner with a needle in my chest port and constant infusions being pumped into my body. The port was about the size of a quarter, relatively flat, and was inserted just beneath the skin. Its purpose was to ease the injection process; rather than insert an IV into my veins for every chemo treatment, the nurse would simply puncture the skin with an approximately one-inch needle, insert it directly into the port, and thus eliminate the need to find a vein.

The chemo room consisted of about twenty chairs, set up in rows with most chairs facing the windows, although there was one row of chairs backed up to the windows and facing all the other chairs in the room. These chairs were not desirable, and if I got stuck in this row, it would be a long day. After all, isn't it always about getting the best seat? And the best view in this room was looking out—away, through the window.

Most patients were quiet, although some would strike up a conversation. Usually, I would select a chair in the back row, facing the windows, as for the most part I wasn't a very social chemo patient. I brought my snacks and a book—always a biography of someone who interested me—and I was content for several hours, as long as there were few delays in the process.

Many patients had lost their hair and many were gaunt and frail. I started the process with hair but would lose it all somewhere around the third chemo treatment. I was typical: I lost not only the hair on my head, but also just about every hair on my body, including my eyebrows. For the second time in my life I was bald, and again I was somewhat self-conscious about the huge scar on my head.

Some patients would successfully complete their treatments, while others were not as fortunate. The nurses would routinely make their rounds, changing IV bags, checking pumps, providing blankets and juice bottles, and offering encouragement. Most patients would sleep. I tried to sleep but could only nod off periodically, because as soon as I would drift off, my right leg would start twitching, waking me up.

It was weird, almost as though my first medical condition—the one that started with a numb foot—was screaming, "Hey, don't forget about me! I was your first!" This happened during every chemo treatment. I would later discover, from conversations with my neurosurgeon, that this involuntary twitching of a muscle or a group of muscles is known as a hypnic jerk and is common for people to encounter while falling asleep. Although likely somehow related to my brain surgery, it was not a seizure. That was good news; however, the occurrence was bad news for getting any sleep during eight hours of chemotherapy!

I read, but many times it was hard to focus. I would have liked to snack throughout the day, but I never had much of an appetite and the chemo had a way of making everything taste like dirt. As a result, I just spent the time looking at people.

Chapter 34

Man Hands

I WILL ALWAYS REMEMBER ONE MAN who was getting treatment. My best guess is that he was in his fifties; he was a black man approximately six feet in height, slender, and bald from the chemotherapy. He showed up every Monday, the same day as my schedule, approximately one hour after I arrived.

As he took his chair, usually one on the east wall closest to the nurse's station, he continually spoke to patients in adjacent chairs and to the nurses. He encouraged the patients, repeatedly telling them, "We all can beat this!" He knew many by name, but I never sat close enough to him to give him an opportunity to strike up a conversation or develop a friendship with me, so he never knew mine. He chatted up the nurses and never had a negative word to say. After a few hours he would cover himself with a blanket and nod off to sleep.

Most patients enjoyed his conversations and positive energy, though I could sense that a few were somewhat irritated and wanted to be left alone. I was fine with him. He was entertaining, and since I was unable to sleep, he helped pass the time.

Lyn took me to the first few treatments, as she had done two years earlier, and would pull up a chair next to me. She would bring a book to read or crossword puzzles to solve. Because my treatments lasted seven to eight hours, she would leave around lunchtime and bring back food; however, my appetite was limited. I tried to drink juice and at least eat half a sandwich, but food and beverages had lost all taste for me. I'd always been a diehard soft-drink consumer, but now, I could not stomach the taste of sodas. I don't think I drank a soft drink for at least six months. I ate only enough to maintain my energy. Often my lunch comprised solely a Jamba Juice smoothie with blended bananas, strawberries, and of course an energy boost. It felt and sounded healthy.

After the first two treatments, just like during my previous go-round, it seemed unnecessary to me for Lyn to be driving me to treatments and sitting around all day. I may have to spend my time this way, I reasoned, but why should she waste her day? She wanted to come, but I urged her to tend to her work and errands, which seemed much more logical. So I began driving myself to treatments every three weeks, bringing a few snacks to try to eat during the day.

Briana came once, too, and stayed with me for about four hours. It gave her a visual of the entire process, which was better than any explanation I could provide. She asked about a young woman, who appeared no older than thirty and was wearing a bandana to cover her hairless head. She asked about the elderly man who slept the entire morning, despite the fact (or maybe because of the fact!) that his wife was faithfully sitting by his side, holding his hand the whole time. She asked, finally, about the younger, hairless man who remained wide awake and constantly scanned the room, looking at every patient, and who appeared astonished that this was happening to him. I had few answers. I never conversed with enough patients to find out who had cancer, who was receiving dialysis treatments, or who was terminally ill.

At one point during my treatment, my port refused to cooperate. Its purpose was to simplify the process, enabling a single insertion of a needle, but this time my port decided it was going to move around under my skin, causing the nurses to insert and remove the needle over and over until they finally found the port's opening. After a second chemo session during which I felt like a human pincushion, I was sent to the hospital for an examination of my port.

The surgical radiologists had me lie down on a table. While using an x-ray scope, they proceeded to stick me with needles repeatedly in an attempt to stabilize the port. "This is extremely rare," they said. "We're not sure why your radiologist surgeon installed this type of port." I just lay there thinking, "Well, this figures . . . rarity is my specialty!"

Throughout the chemotherapy process, I continued to meet periodically with my oncologist. During one appointment, he scheduled me to visit the City of Hope, a department in a nearby hospital that primarily dealt with bone marrow transplants when all else had failed. "All else" meant the chemo treatments. "Failed" meant the chemo had been ineffective in killing the cancer. I was reluctant, but I ended up going anyway, almost out of curiosity more than anything else.

Lyn went with me, and we met with a physician who spent about an hour explaining how a bone marrow transplant would take place, if I needed one. She explained a complex process, but what really stuck with me was that I would have about a 10 percent chance of dying from the bone marrow transplant. Now, 10 percent is usually a low percentage, but when it represents the odds of your death, it suddenly seems very high.

Still, I found myself listening less and less to what she was saying and focusing more and more on how big her hands were.

Don't get me wrong, she was obviously a seasoned specialist physician, and extremely attractive to boot; however, I kept thinking about that *Seinfeld* episode—the one where Jerry dated a woman with "man hands." I mentioned this to Lyn.

"So, we just spent an hour discussing a bone marrow transplant as a last resort to save your life if the chemotherapy doesn't work, and all you can talk about is her 'man hands'?" she exclaimed.

"I know, I know," I said, then added: "But weren't they abnormally large for such an attractive woman?"

Chapter 35

Deal with It

TO PREPARE FOR THE UNCERTAIN FUTURE— the one that might include the dreaded bone marrow transplant—I would have to have a bone marrow biopsy first. Naturally. Here we go again.

My oncologist said I would be required to check in to the hospital, put on a gown, wait in a room, and finally have the biopsy under anesthesia—all this despite the fact that it was an outpatient procedure. I'd long since passed any level of patience with all this stuff, so I asked if there were any other options. Please, I thought, don't make me put the gown on again!

He did say he could perform the biopsy in his office, though that was unusual, but I would receive only a shot to help numb some of the pain. In other words, the pain would be significant if I chose this option.

Not a problem, doc. Sign me up.

So, we scheduled an in-office biopsy appointment, and when the day arrived, I figured, "How bad could it be?"

I lay down on my side, the nurse gave me a few shots to numb my hip area, and then I was told my doctor would be inserting an instrument deep into my hip, which would cut through the bone and retrieve a small chunk of marrow. OK... not exactly what I was expecting, but we were there, I thought, so let's get it done.

The instrument was thrust far into my hip, and I could feel and hear a scraping and cutting of the bone; it felt as though something was reaching deep into the core of my body, causing a very bizarre pain.

The nurse looked at me and said, "Are you OK? You look like you're smiling."

And, later, as I walked out of my oncologist's office having avoided the ad nauseam details associated with going to the hospital, the anesthesia, and having to put a gown on, I thought, "Piece of cake. Things could have gone much, much worse!"

With the biopsy done in case of a worst-case scenario, I continued on with my chemotherapy. The two weeks following each session were always pretty bad. Not only did I ultimately lose all the hair on my body, but also I lost about fifteen pounds (hey, maybe I should have found the idiot neurologist and asked him if I was now fit to run a marathon), and generally walked around feeling weak, nauseated, and lifeless.

But I worked every day. Showing up was merely my way of moving on with life and focusing on planning for my postchemo, postcancer life. It was just something I had to do. I even managed to take on a new and challenging project. I sat in my office one day, casually speaking with Ben, a senior appraiser who had worked at the firm for four years and was close to receiving his MAI—the equivalent for appraisers of the CPA designation for accountants.

Ben is about six feet two inches tall and rock solid in build, and he was a former collegiate athlete who had trained for the 2004 Olympics as a decathlete. Since he had trained at the University of Texas–Austin, we talked about Texas and how I had always dreamed of opening an additional appraisal office in Austin. My dad ended his Air Force career in Austin, and I lived there for eleven years, including graduating from the University of Texas. Ultimately, Ben said, "Why didn't you mention this before . . . my wife and I have always thought about living in Austin." Further conversations led to Ben moving to Austin and heading up the new office as regional manager.

In that initial discussion, we continued to iron out the details but agreed (basically on my recommendation) to wait and open up the new office in early 2009. By then I would have completed all chemotherapy and radiation.

Most of my friends and colleagues couldn't understand why I would be planning an expansion of the Phoenix operation—a new office in a different state—when I had cancer, was undergoing chemotherapy, and for the most part felt like throwing up just about every waking moment of the day. My answer, once again, was that I never really expected nor planned to die; rather, I planned to keep on living and planning for the future, past cancer.

My staff saw me every day, but I revealed little about the

pain or sickness I felt. They probably all assumed the chemo wasn't affecting me the way it affected "normal" people—after all, when I'd had the brain tumor, they'd seen me seem to recuperate so quickly.

While I may have looked like a ninety-year-old man, my temperament and energy appeared relatively normal, even when I felt like crap. I never let on about the waves of nausea, the random bloody noses, the headaches, stomach cramps, bowel movement problems, heartburn, or the overall feeling of death I experienced to varying degrees day in and day out. In my mind, it wasn't their problem and it certainly wouldn't have made the scenario any better for them or for the company if they had been aware. Only Al and Jessica knew the entire story, but they also understood that I wanted it kept private. I had discovered Monster coffee drinks, my favorite of which was "Mean Bean." Essentially, they were energy drinks. They taste awesome, my stomach didn't reject them, and they gave me energy to work through the day. Co-workers questioned, "Should you be drinking energy drinks while on chemo?" I responded, "Yes, I believe I should!"

As part of my daily routine, during every shower, I would recite to myself a simple phrase: "Washing away all tumors and cancer. Washing away all tumors and cancer." I repeated it. I even created a jingle, a tune, to accompany the words, and I sang it to myself every time I stepped in the shower.

The mind has incredible power, and it was my definitive goal to tap every unknown healing source located somewhere in my brain, either conscious or unconscious. The jingle became my morning motto. I would convince my subconscious being as well as my conscious self that I was actually washing away the evil cells.

I'd repeat the words, slightly modified, each night when I got into bed. The before-bed phrase included language that while I was sleeping, my body would be working to kill, eliminate, and abolish all cancer and tumor cells.

Hey, some people count sheep to put themselves to sleep. Me? I counted the ways to keep myself alive.

I did my best to keep up with my family life as well. Near the end of Briana's five-week internship, Olivia and I flew to Chicago for Briana's last four or five days at Northwestern University. The intern program concluded with students performing all of the plays they had produced and rehearsed in those five weeks. Briana's play was performed twice during this week. Since Briana last had seen me, I had lost all of my hair and quite a bit of weight. During one of our shopping sprees in Chicago, I bought a blue pullover shirt, which was rather trendy and most likely more appropriate for a younger, more hip man. However, I hadn't been that thin in about twenty years. Near the end of our trip I donned the shirt, looking very thin and trendy. I was bald, had nearly lost my eyebrows, and was beginning to look somewhat gaunt in the face, but I proudly wore that shirt!

While the new blue shirt fit well, my existing clothes fit rather loosely because of the amount of weight I had lost. In the porte cochere of the hotel, while I was loading our luggage into the taxi, my shorts dropped! The shorts were so loose on my waist that they fell completely to my ankles, exposing my boxer briefs to the entire world, or at least anyone who cared to watch. The taxi driver stood speechless, and I was so shocked that I actually stood there for a few seconds before I desperately grabbed my shorts and pulled them back up. Briana was standing directly next to me and burst into laughter.

Lyn and I toward the end of my chemotherapy. I'm smiling 'cause my hair is coming back!

After only four treatments of the eight I'd originally been scheduled for, three months into chemotherapy, a scan revealed that the mass was completely gone. My oncologist was surprised, to say the least. But my radiologist—the one who'd treated me during my brain tumor days—was less surprised.

Had I been blessed by a miracle and given a second—wait, I suppose that would be a third—chance in life? Was it the wonder of medicine whereby the chemotherapy had actually deteriorated a fourteen-centimeter mass in only four treatments, when my oncologist had forecast that a minimum of eight would be necessary?

Had my willpower and positive belief actually "washed away" the cancer?

Or was it a combination of all of the above?

Who knows? The doctors certainly didn't hazard a guess, and, to be on the safe side, my oncologist wanted me to finish at least six treatments and plan for several weeks of radiation thereafter. As much as I wanted to end the sickness, the nausea, the lack of appetite, and the total lack of energy, I agreed to two more treatments. My final chemotherapy treatment took place on a Monday toward the end of October 2008, and I never again visited the City of Hope.

I suppose I should have celebrated the results that said I was cancer free; however, since the day I'd been told I had cancer, I had always believed in miracles. I had believed in the power of medicine, and I had always believed in my will to fight. I was unbelievably grateful the cancerous mass was gone, but I wasn't completely surprised.

As I left my oncologist's office that day, I called my family to report the results and I headed back to work.

Business as usual.

Chapter 36

The Nonissue of Commitment

EARLIER IN THE YEAR, a friend of mine had become engaged. Dave and I met in 1986 and had maintained our friendship for over twenty years. I was a groomsman in his first wedding, in 1994, he was a groomsman in my wedding with Lyn, and in early 2008 he had once again asked me to be a groomsman. I not only had accepted, but also had offered our house for a postreception party.

Our house was designed by Will Bruder, a contemporary architect, and built in 1986. The house is circular and constructed of concrete-block exterior walls and patina copper panels. As an architecturally unique home, it is an excellent party house, with views of nearby mountains and a multiple-tiered backyard with a concrete fire pit, a swimming pool with a waterfall, and a spa. Many have said it looks like a water tank or have asked us why we would want to live in a house that looks like an office building. It definitely fits into the category of "love it or hate it." We love it.

View of our "circle" house

The wedding was scheduled for November 1, and when Dave heard of my cancer in mid-2008, he told me I should in no way feel obligated to attend his wedding or to hold the postreception party at our house. Nevertheless, throughout my chemo treatments I told Dave I planned on being in his wedding, regardless of my appearance, and that the party would go on. When November 1 arrived, I had finished my six chemo treatments and was in the early stages of radiation treatment. As a result, I was thin, gaunt, bald, and nearly hairless otherwise as well. I only hoped that I didn't draw any attention away from Dave and Deborah, his bride, because of pity. The wedding went smoothly, and we were gratified when more than seventy people showed up at our house for the after-party.

The drinks were flowing, a fire was blazing, music was playing, and the pool waterfall was streaming. People were touring the house inside and out. Dave was overwhelmed when he saw Jessica bartending, having come to know her through the years. About halfway through the party, I broke out a poem.

At the rehearsal dinner the previous night, Lyn and I had met Deborah's family, and I was reacquainted with several of Dave's family members whom I had met over the years. Because I wrote the poem the day of the wedding—I seem to write better under pressure—these people became the focus of the poem, and since the wedding date was approaching Christmastime, I based the poem on *The Night Before Christmas*. Further, Dave attended Penn State University and is an absolutely fanatical football fan. The poem read as follows.

'Twas the night before the wedding, when all through the church,

Not a pastor was preaching, or a sermon in search;

The candles were perched, waiting to be lit,

The pews in their position for the people to sit;

Both Deborah and Dave were asleep in their beds,

While visions of the wedding night danced in their heads;

And Nana in her nightgown and Ray not making a peep,

Had just settled down for a long night sleep;

When out of the TV there came a sound,

Dave sprang from the bed to see who was around;

Into the living room he strolled at a pace,

Scratched his head and put his hand to his face;

As what to his wondering eyes would appear,

But Max at the TV holding a beer;

Max ranted and raved and shouted in frustration,

The Penn State game was rescheduled; this is not a good situation;

Iowa's in town, they're playing tomorrow,

Dave's face went blank and was filled with sorrow;

Nancy entered the room saying, "What's the matter?

I can't get to sleep with all this chatter!"

Then into the crowd Paul came with a bound,

Dazed and confused why everyone was around;

"It's 3:00 in the morning, what's wrong with you people?

The wedding's tomorrow, we're all going to be feeble!"

Then with a wink of his eye and a twist of his head,

Max started to explain the story Dave would dread;

"Penn State plays tomorrow, we have to watch them play;

The game has been moved up and the wedding will be another day;

They're on their way to Miami—a national championship,

There's no room for a wedding, Dave—don't give me no lip;

We'll have to replan it, far, far away,

Maybe February, March, April, or May";

Dave hemmed and hawed and said, "I think I feel sick;

Deborah's not going to be happy—plus she's the best wife I've picked";

He covered his eyes with his hands, distraught,

An ideal situation this surely was not;

Then Lance started shaking him: "Dave, snap out of it,

You're having a nightmare and throwing a fit;

You're marrying my mom today, it's already noon,

You've been sleeping all morning, the wedding is soon!"

Dave sighed in relief and realized he could still watch his team,

The game is next week and this was all just a dream.

During the after-party, I rarely thought of my sour stomach or my lack of energy; rather, I could think only of what I would have missed if I had taken the easy road and backed out of the wedding or the party because of my physical state. Everyone would have understood, Lyn would have supported my decision, and it would have been the obvious choice. However, it would have been the wrong decision. Dave's wedding, the outdoor reception, and the postreception party at our house are memories I will carry for the rest of my life.

Radiation treatments would last five weeks. I wanted to start immediately, as our company Christmas party was scheduled for mid-December and I wanted to feel normal and possibly have a little bit of hair on my head. Once again, I didn't want the focus of the party to be my illness; the less physical evidence, the better.

Again I pleaded with the nurses to schedule me in the early morning so I could get my butt into the office. Since I had my same radiologist, and his staff all remembered me from a few years earlier, little persuasion was necessary. The radiation covered a "field" on my chest, and it was delivered through both my chest and my back, in an effort to kill any cancer cells that might have survived chemotherapy.

By year's end in 2008, my company had posted a record, with slightly greater than $2.8 million in gross revenues. Lefevers Viewpoint Group, Inc. was listed by *Inc. Magazine* as one of the 5,000 fastest-growing private companies in America (we were listed way at the bottom, as number 4,725, but we still made the list).

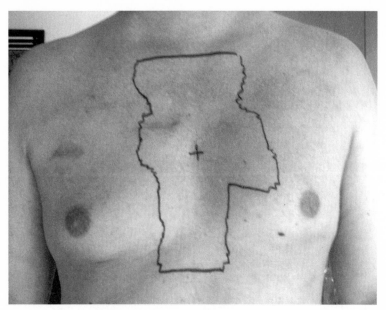

Radiation "field" and scars/bruises from port, surgeries, and biopsies

For the year-end Christmas party, we continued the out-of-town tradition and set off for Anaheim, where we stayed at Disneyland's Grand Californian hotel. Employees were invited to bring their entire families, and each employee was given two "hopper" passes to Disneyland and California Adventure.

For our predinner happy hour, we hired Mickey Mouse to attend our party for about half an hour. Let's just say Mickey is not cheap; Mickey shows up with a bodyguard. A bodyguard who made absolutely sure that Mickey did not appear in any photographs that involved alcohol. All employees' children who had made the trip were invited to take pictures with Mickey. And Mickey didn't hesitate to sit down and play games with the kids; however, he never spoke.

Our company game was "Who Wants to Be a \$250 Winner," a slight deviation from *Who Wants to Be a Millionaire?*, and I roasted two employees: John, a senior appraiser, and Jessica. Both had been with the company for five years.

The highlight of Jessica's roast was a wallet that, when I opened it up, contained a plastic photograph holder with fifty photos of men; I implied, of course, that she had dated all of these men during her five-year tenure with the company, as she remained one of the few single employees. In reality she had only dated a few, but the photographs were real and I named the men one by one, leaving some to seriously wonder if my story held some truth. My roast of John culminated with a letter from one of our top clients (a woman). Throughout the year she had regularly requested John for specific appraisal assignments and had reported the quality of his appraisal reports coupled with his excellent service and cooperativeness during the review process. The letter read as follows:

John:

When Jay told me he was "roasting" you for your five years of tenure, I asked if I could write a short note. During these difficult times of the economy, and particularly within the banking industry, the appraisal department of [my bank] has made a conscious choice to tighten our requirements of appraisal reports and to become more selective of individual appraisers we utilize. Since these changes were implemented, you have become one of my top appraisers, due to the quality and timeliness of your reports.

Further, your personal service has been unprecedented. You are always pleasant and cooperative on the phone, as your voice impacts me like a persuasive purr. I have also appreciated your personal delivery of reports. The first time you delivered a report, my heart actually fluttered, my spine tingled, and my mind screamed danger. I had to hold myself back from giving in to your charm as my body quivered. As you handed me the report, our hands touched and my skin burned under the light caress.

I am now hopelessly torn between my own secret desires and the certain knowledge you view me only as a client. When I receive your e-mails my heart hammers in my chest, my stomach contracts, and tremors run down my thighs. But I now understand that extraordinary circumstances had brought about this connection and it had to end . . . yet I continue to request you for appraisal assignments, based solely, of course, on the quality of your work. Congratulations on your five years with Lefevers Viewpoint Group, Inc.!

The room was silent for the first few moments of the reading of the letter; most employees knew of this client's favoritism toward John, so the letter was believable, to start. Some were awed that a client would take the time to write such kind words. However, as my recitation of the letter progressed and the language headed for the gutter, all realized it was part of a typical "Jay" roasting, and the room subsequently filled with laughter; I had to pause numerous times, waiting for the laughter to subside.

Because of my health, I never formed a baseball "club" team; however, I continued to keep in touch with Jonathan, Preston, E-man, and Angel. Jonathan was working, and we periodically kept in touch via texting; further, he would come by the house every few months and continued to keep his promise not to deal drugs. Every six months or so, Jonathan would work for me—helping me move furniture in the office, doing landscape work around the house or office, and the like. Preston was in his senior year of high school, playing tennis and baseball. Lyn and I went to see him in the state finals for doubles tennis, and our entire family went to a few of his baseball games. We heard from E-man and Angel less frequently. E-man reportedly didn't finish high school, but he said he received his GED. He worked at a grocery store, and we stopped by a few times to see him. He was surprised we went out of our way to see him, and always grateful; I only wished we could do more. Angel finished high school. He played baseball his senior year and was the starting shortstop. We went to see him play twice, and he always appreciated that we took the time to attend his games. Again, I felt as though there must be more I could do.

Chapter 37

You're Very Fortunate

THE YEAR 2009 WAS MY HEALTHIEST in five years. However, because of the economic decline, it proved to be the toughest year for my appraisal business.

The national recession and bursting of the real estate bubble, which had commenced in 2007, had a substantial impact in 2008 and 2009 on all real estate related companies, including brokerage firms, title companies, and, unfortunately, real estate appraisal companies. My company had weathered the storm relatively well during 2007 and 2008. However, the effect finally trickled our way in 2009. To further exacerbate this scenario, I decided to take on even more risk, and incur more expenses toward marketing, commencing in 2009. I knew I was going against the grain, but I believed that these steps would better position my company for the future.

Ben and I opened the Austin office in February 2009. In addition, in September 2008 I had entered into a contract to acquire a 16,500-square-foot, multi-tenant office building in Phoenix, of which the lower level would house my appraisal company and the upper level would be leased to multiple office tenants. Acquisition of this building would close escrow in January 2009. In other words, during the worst real estate recession in thirty-plus years, I was buying an office building, opening a new regional appraisal office by relocating one of my top-billing appraisers, increasing marketing expenses, and moving the company's physical location. I wasn't just going against the grain—I was operating on sandpaper. Smart business? Maybe so, maybe not, but I refused to stand still.

Soon after the Austin office opened, Ben and I mutually decided to relocate him back to Phoenix, where his kids were ingrained in their school system and the environment was better for his family. Consequently, I would spend the latter half of 2009 performing numerous Texas appraisal assignments myself (while Ben picked up a few to help out). Simultaneously, I was scouring the Texas market for a new regional manager—Ben's replacement. I tried hiring a local (Austin) appraiser to keep the office open, but it did not work out. We ended up shutting down the Austin office in 2010. I had briefly accomplished my dream of opening an office in Texas; we had given it a valiant effort, but it was ultimately shattered. Again, I was reminded of a simple concept in business: while your people are your greatest asset, they can also become your utmost liability.

Conversely, the acquisition of the office building was extremely successful. The Phoenix operation now had a very vibrant and professional environment where we could pursue the future of the company. Our office was architecturally unique, exuded character, and provided space for future expansion if needed. We decorated the walls with eclectic wall hangings and artwork, most of which Lyn and I had collected from our antiques business. Pieces included midcentury paintings, vintage contemporary clocks, an eye-shaped mirror, a very large Orange Crush bottle cap, and a vintage metal sign that says "We Give Orange Stamps." The sign has absolutely no relevance to the appraisal business; however, it was orange, the company color. Further, the building was centrally located, providing access to all areas of metropolitan Phoenix.

I had won one and I had lost one. At whatever cost, I was batting .500; I'll take it any season.

Still, 2009 was challenging. Year-end revenues dropped to near $2.4 million. It was much easier to operate a growing, thriving, profitable company than a shrinking one. During 2009 I worked more hours, scrambled harder to generate business, spent more money marketing the company, and took home far, far less money. In fact, the annual net profit was nominal, allowing me to take only a token salary. If I was in town, I was at the office seven days a week; I thought about the business twenty-four hours a day: "What could I do differently?" "How can I better prepare for 2010?"

On numerous occasions throughout the year, the account balance was insufficient to make payroll. So I plunged more of my personal money into the company, and Al and I performed creative tactics. We always paid all of our vendors, and we always did make payroll, somehow, someway. Employees never knew of the company's financial strife. It wasn't their burden. I took pride in the company's ability to endure the tenuous year and the fact that I never laid off a single employee. I may have fired someone for poor performance, but not a single employee lost his or her job because of the company's substantial decline in revenues.

In spite of the fragile financial year, I chose again to continue the out-of-town party tradition. The company couldn't afford an elaborate year-end party, but I spent some of my personal funds to make it happen. I wondered if I was sending the wrong message to employees. Would I rather they assume, based on the out-of-town party, that the company was financially sound? Or was it more beneficial to shoot straight with employees and explain why a cheaper, scaled-down year-end party was necessary? I chose to buffer employees from the company's financial friction.

We chose San Antonio as the destination for our outing. As usual, we had a fantastic time roasting a couple of our hardest-working employees and playing a version of *The Match Game*. Once again the game got a little out of control, a little raunchy, with some outrageous answers coming from the spouses and significant others. Of course it was a whole lot of fun.

My radiation treatment wasn't fun, but I survived. After it concluded, I had severe damage to the tissue surrounding my lungs, which caused inflammation and difficulty breathing. I would be short of breath even after climbing a simple flight of stairs or when I lay on my back, and my constant coughing might have suggested that I smoked four or five packs of cigarettes a day. It didn't help matters that I was completely out of shape, as I had hardly exercised in more than a year.

My pulmonary specialist gave me an extensive breathing exam that lasted about forty-five minutes and revealed that my breathing capacity was about 70 percent. Apparently, because of the severe tissue damage, I likely would have to live with this symptom for the rest of my life.

"You could live with this breathing capacity until about age 125," my specialist said.

"OK, as long as you're still around as my doctor," I replied.

Yes, my pulmonary specialist was separate from my oncologist, my radiologist, my neurologist, and my neurosurgeon. I was surrounded by specialists, which made me feel, well, "special."

Although they might not help, my pulmonary specialist still decided to put me on steroids to attempt to reduce the inflammation. I was ready to get built, look buff, and regain the physique I had (or at least that I remember having) when I was in my twenties. However, these characteristics were side effects of anabolic steroids, the kind professional athletes often are accused of taking, which are chemically derived from testosterone. My steroid was Prednisone, or a corticosteroid, which comprises a group of man-made hormones that have a cortisone-like action. Cortisone is produced naturally in the body and is involved in regulating inflammation.

Potential side effects associated with Prednisone include increased blood sugar, weight gain, facial swelling, depression, psychosis, mania, fatigue, mental confusion, blurred vision, abdominal pain, peptic ulcer, infections, migraines, insomnia, cataracts, anxiety, stomach pain, mouth sores, nervousness, acne, rashes, diarrhea . . . What the hell? I don't want all this shit. I'll just take the inflammation and shortness of breath!

It's like those commercials on television where the announcer quickly rambles over a series of potential side effects, each of which sounds like an illness itself. Nevertheless, I agreed to take the steroids, which were to be prescribed for at least a six-month period. Among the side effects I actually experienced were extensive weight gain, rashes, and mental confusion . . . or maybe the mental confusion was merely an element of my personality!

With the steroids in full effect, I weighed about 215 pounds, or at least 20 to 25 pounds overweight. As a result, I had little desire to exercise and I was always thinking about the magnitude of other side effects. Was I fatigued? Was I mentally confused? Was I anxious? If so, was it because of the steroids, or other factors? I had too many questions and no clear-cut answers. Overall, I needed to lose the steroids. So, I wrote myself a prescription, unbeknownst to my doctor, and cut my dosage in half.

In a matter of weeks, my shortness of breath and wheezing came back, about twice as bad as they had been immediately after the radiation. A visit to my pulmonary specialist revealed why. Once he had recovered from his astonishment when I explained that I had reduced my dosage without instruction from him or from my oncologist, he calmly reported the severe risk associated with such a reduction and the reasons dosages were to be slowly reduced.

Effectively, my drastic cut in dosage caused a recurrence of my inflammation, and to a greater degree than before. Lesson learned: When it comes to medication, never self-prescribe. My new prescription was to go back on steroids; I was basically starting over and would now need to stay on the steroids for no less than six more months. Jay the puffy fat-ass was back, and so were the other side effects from the steroids. I was fatigued, I would experience periodic severe abdominal pain, and rashes would randomly appear on my body. But this time I followed the prescription instructions to a T.

Chapter 38

Breathing in Paradise

THE BREATHING DIFFICULTIES PREVENTED me even from simply walking around the block. Lyn and I would occasionally take evening walks, but I would have to stop every hundred feet or so just to catch my breath. I once again thought of the simplicities in life that many of us take for granted; though I now had become accustomed to walking with a numb foot and leg, I faced yet another challenge: merely having the aerobic ability to walk a short distance.

However, my doctor indicated that the exercise should eventually help to improve my lung capacity; therefore, two to three times per week, we walked, and walked, always stopping for Jay to catch his breath. The distances were short, but I had high hopes.

The abdominal cramps surfaced only periodically, but

when a severe pain would hit, the heartburn was so intense that I truly thought, "So, this is how it feels to have a heart attack?" On a few occasions I was doubled over, in my office, waiting and waiting for the pain to subside. It wouldn't have done any good for me to go home; the pain had no concern for location, as it basically emerged whenever and wherever it chose. Eventually it would go away, waiting for another day to come out and play.

The multiple doctor's visits continued to try my patience. During one routine visit to my oncologist I spent a total of an hour and a half waiting in the lobby, waiting after my blood was drawn, and again waiting in the little exam room for my oncologist. Eventually, I got up, left the little room, told the nurse I was done for the day, and went back to work. My oncologist's office called me there and asked what happened. I replied, "I had an appointment and it wasn't kept."

The next time I went to the office, I didn't have to wait very long. My tactic worked.

During the summer of 2009, our family tradition of visiting a different state continued, but we finally ended the tradition of attending a professional baseball game or touring a university (or both). We spent the last week of July in Honolulu, Hawaii. The last time I checked, Honolulu did not have a professional baseball team, and we didn't end up touring any colleges or universities. Olivia didn't join us on this trip, as she had decided to become a youth ambassador that summer, following in Adam's footsteps. Olivia had a three-week trip to Ireland, then hosted her Irish counterpart for three weeks in the United States.

Our Hawaii excursions included parasailing in the ocean, a ride through the forest-covered mountains on ATVs, a bus tour of movie settings across the island, a tour of Pearl Harbor, a dinner cruise, of course plenty of shopping, a boat ride to visit the dolphins, and, finally, snorkeling.

I had grown up riding a motorcycle in the desert and therefore found the ATV tour to be memorable. In spite of the fact that we were required to maintain a certain (slow) speed and had to ride in a single-file line, as the caboose of our group I was able to perform a few fishtails when the guide wasn't looking. Plus, Adam, who was in front of me, kept me fully entertained by continually bumping into Briana . . . accidentally, I'm sure. We rode through absolutely incredible terrain, and at one point my only thought was to thank God for allowing me to be on that ATV, at that particular moment, with my family, in Hawaii. I did have to buy some closed-toe shoes, which the tour company recommended for riding ATVs, as all I had brought to Hawaii were (open-toe) sandals. Because my closed-toe shoes were brand new, they were bright white; further, they gave me giant blisters on my ankles.

Our next venture was a one-day, self-guided tour of the island, which provided all indications of a total disaster in the offing, primarily because of Jay's master plan. Somehow I assumed we could jump in our rental jeep, tour Pearl Harbor in the morning, and complete a drive around the entire island during the remainder of the day, including stopping at the Dole Plantation, grabbing some world-famous "shave ice" at Matsumoto in the town of Haleiwa, taking a break at the North Shore for a dip in the ocean, and spending the evening at the Polynesian Cultural Center. Needless to say, we had to rush through our itinerary to fit everything in, especially after we spent several hours waiting for the shave ice at Matsumoto. We skipped the Dole Plantation and showed up too late to tour the Polynesian Center.

Adam, Lyn, some idiot in bright white shoes, and Briana

Our most memorable stop wasn't on the itinerary at all. On the North Shore, we found a small beach without a soul in sight. We pulled the jeep over, headed for the water, and decided we would spend only about half an hour walking the beach and wading in the water so we could still make it to the Polynesian Cultural Center to relax, eat dinner, and spend the rest of the evening. But we spent nearly two hours at the beach, absolutely obsessed with taking "jumping" pictures—photographs of us jumping into the air on the beach. Sounds easy, but it wasn't, although it was a great deal of fun.

The next day, our snorkeling adventure commenced with a long boat ride out onto the ocean, during which several dolphins seemed to enjoy swimming alongside the boat. Approximately thirty people were on the boat, including tourists from all over the world, from small kids to grandmothers and grandfathers. The plan was to ride out for about an hour, to an area where turtles, manta rays, and exotic fish resided, at which point the boat would shut down and we would be allowed to snorkel for about forty-five minutes.

We were instructed how to wear the snorkel mask and flippers and were given an inflatable vest to keep us afloat while we snorkeled. One by one the tourists lowered themselves into the water or took a plunge off the side of the boat. Lyn, Briana, and Adam were in the water ahead of me, so I jumped feetfirst into the water and came up kicking so I could catch up to them.

Immediately, I noticed a shortness of breath, so I stopped kicking. The air restriction wasn't improving, so I removed my mask to help my breathing and inflated my vest to enable myself to stay afloat without kicking or treading water. Nothing helped. In fact, I soon found myself gasping for air. Immersing myself in water had apparently compressed my lungs, which, coupled with my already reduced breathing capacity, resulted in a near inability to breathe.

I later learned that such "dyspnea" is a common symptom in patients with diaphragm weakness or paralysis. In particular, dyspnea may be aggravated by immersion to the neck in water. Scrambling back to the boat as best as I could, I waved off Lyn and told her to go on without me. Of course, she did the opposite and swam back to the boat. Meanwhile, Briana and Adam had no idea what was going on.

I pulled myself up and poured myself onto the deck of the boat. Again, I waved to Lyn to go on, as I couldn't get enough air to speak. Knowing me, she headed out to catch up with Briana and Adam. However, seeing that I was having trouble breathing, a lifeguard (who was also a tour guide on the boat) and the boat's captain were standing over me, asking what was wrong and threatening to call a safety boat for me. Once I caught my breath, I convinced them I would be just fine and told them I had recently recovered from lymphoma, a form of cancer, and that my shortness of breath was probably a result of the chemotherapy and radiation, which severely reduced my lung capacity. After their concern lessened, they asked why I would even attempt snorkeling. I continued to remove my vest and my flippers but did not directly answer that question.

For the rest of the snorkeling adventure, I remained on the boat and watched Lyn, Briana, Adam, and all of the other tourists swim about with turtles and exotic fish. After about ten minutes I stopped feeling sorry for myself and hit the bar on the boat. The lifeguard made me a drink and told me story after story about idiot tourists. I'm pretty sure I had just become one of her future stories; however, I enjoyed myself as much as possible and had another drink. "What's the big deal with snorkeling anyway?" I thought. I was sitting on a boat in the middle of the ocean, off the Hawaiian Islands, with a drink in my hand, talking to a young female tour guide wearing a bikini. Life was good.

Chapter 39

Family First

IN THE FALL OF 2009, my family would venture to Marina del Rey, California, to drop off Briana at Loyola Marymount University. We spent nearly three days moving her into her dorm room, attending seminars, touring the campus, buying T-shirts, and eating.

The final moments of the trip were extremely difficult. Briana and I cried as we left each other's arms, and it was tough to drive away, leaving my daughter in another state, where she didn't know a soul. I knew she was starting another chapter in her life, a chapter that would not involve me nearly as much as I'd been involved for the previous eighteen years. I had raised her to be independent, and independent she was.

The thought of possibly not having been around for this experience crossed my mind. Taking her to college was one more once in a lifetime opportunity; I was thankful to be around to see my daughter start her collegiate career.

Drop-off weekend at Loyola Marymount University; the Overdramatic Lefevers Family

As I've written, Lyn is my second wife, and Adam and Olivia are my stepchildren. Briana's mom and I were divorced when Briana was two years old, and I spent nine years as a single father with 50 percent custody. I'm proud of the years I spent changing diapers, attending plays, meeting with teachers, dressing up as a "pretty princess," and telling bedtime stories; however, I've never felt qualified to give advice about marriages, nor about raising a child.

Earlier, I also worked hard to get through a four-year undergraduate program, during which time I worked for a title company. I also made it through a two-year master's program, and I've busted my butt for nearly two decades to achieve the success my company has accomplished. Yet I also hesitate to give business or career advice.

Finally, I have suffered through severe medical conditions, but I find it hard to advise people on how to deal with their own medical conditions.

Rather, I prefer to listen. I can listen to their marriage problems, their child-raising scenarios, their business or career dilemmas, and their medical conditions, and I can ask a lot of questions. Plus, I can give ideas, generally examples from my life, as to how I've worked hard to maintain a positive attitude through two marriages, through raising one daughter and two stepchildren, through many business successes and failures, and during two life-threatening medical conditions. Most people will answer my questions and ultimately "talk out" their scenarios, deciding for themselves whether my ideas are pertinent to them or if my life examples are situations they are comfortable implementing in their own lives. This book includes such examples and ideas.

I have earmarked 2009 as the end of an era, the end of my severe medical complications. However, the irony is that this period of my life was filled with so many unforgettable memories: the tribulations and successes of our Little League baseball teams; witnessing Briana perform onstage; the opportunities to attempt new business ventures, including valuable lessons learned from failures as well as successes; trips and vacations; parties; and meeting new people who would change my life.

I would have none of these memories if I had given up on life or taken the "easy road" by standing on the sideline during my medical conditions. I chose to change my point of view, my attitude, my frame of reference, my perspective, or my point of observation. I chose to continue to live for however long God has planned, and to live to my fullest capability during that period. In return, I was blessed with challenges, memories, successes, and failures, and I can look forward to more obstacles and more hurdles throughout the remainder of my life. I continue with a metal plate in my head, a numb right leg and foot, and 70 percent breathing capacity. Many have told me, "You're very fortunate." I am.

If you don't like your current point of view, change it. Turn. Move. Or forge uphill in search of the peak. Regardless, don't stand still.

Post-op

YOU KNOW WHAT THEY SAY, RIGHT? If you survive a life-threatening situation or illness, you're supposed to wake up every morning thereafter, for the rest of your life, feeling refreshed and eager for a brand-new day. You're supposed to notice and appreciate the little things . . . the taste of the takeout turkey sandwich you're having for lunch; the blue, cloudless Arizona sky; the way the air smells after an evening of rainfall; the happy chirps and singing of birds in the early morning. You're supposed to be grateful because, after all, you survived the sleepless nights, the numbness in your limbs, the seizures, the surreality of having your skull opened up, the chemotherapy dripping into your body, the days lost to sitting in hospitals and doctors' offices, the frustration, the fears, and, yes, the sometimes agonizing pain. You're lucky to be alive. After surviving a life-threatening illness, your attitude toward life—toward just being alive—is supposed to be one of constant gratitude and cheer.

This is how everyone expects it to be, how everyone expects you to feel, be, act, and talk after you've survived something others have not.

During five years of fighting for my life, everyone asked me the same questions and made the same comments over and over: "Do you appreciate life more?" "Doesn't life have more meaning for you now?" "Do you have a renewed outlook on life?" "Aren't you more appreciative of the 'small' things in life after what you've been through?"

When asked these questions, especially in the weeks and months following my diagnoses and surgeries, I always responded as the questions were meant to be answered: "Yes, life has become more special"; "Yes, I appreciate each day above ground"; and "Yes, I notice the small things on a daily basis." I knew those were the answers people wanted to hear, and a part of me wanted to give them what they wanted.

My answers always seemed to satisfy the expectations of the people asking the questions, but I felt uncomfortable about it—actually, I was swarmed with feelings of guilt and shame for quite a while. Why *didn't* I feel more appreciative of life and all the "little things" after my illnesses? What was *wrong* with me that I wasn't waking up and bouncing out of bed every morning, grateful just to be alive?

The more I thought about it, the more I realized that the reason I wasn't more appreciative just to be alive after I defied death—twice—was because (news flash): I never expected to die. Never. No way.

My close brushes with potentially deadly circumstances didn't change my appreciation for life for the simple reason that my appreciation for life had always been there.

Because what's small about life? My view on life has always been that everything is big, everything is always pretty important, everything matters, everything is worth doing very well, and everything—or almost everything—is worth trying at least once.

To some people, that perspective has made me a pain-in-the-ass perfectionist. I realize now that it is important to allow others to share in my struggles, both to give them an opportunity to express their love and to help me avoid the resentment I felt when others misunderstood the severity of my condition. To many people, my attitude toward life both before and after my illnesses has made me an inspiration.

My company forges ahead. July 2011 was the company's nineteen-year anniversary. I can't recall much of anything in my life that I have done for nearly twenty years. We survived 2008, 2009, and 2010, years that represent one of the worst real estate recessions in history. My family also has survived. My daughter is twenty years old, and my second wife and I have survived nine years of marriage. I suppose that sometimes survival equals success, both in life and in business!

I keep taking on new projects. In 2010 I formed a new company, JuBiLee Entertainment, LLC (J for Jay, B for Briana, and L for Lyn), which came to own private shares in the first private-equity animation-film fund in the entertainment industry and would invest in *Another Happy Day*, a film starring Ellen Barkin, Demi Moore, Kate Bosworth, Ellen Burstyn, Thomas Haden Church, and George Kennedy, which was released in 2011. No, I didn't get to meet Demi, but my hopes are high!

I have continued to be a coach, but more off the field than on. Jonathan and I have kept in touch on a regular basis, via texting and Facebook, and we see each other on a regular basis—I hired him to provide landscape services for our home and the Phoenix office building. Once, I texted him and asked if he had any input for my book; he responded: "mmm na nt really just hw much of a great team we had, hw much we all cared bout each other n it waz da best team I eva been in . . . dat ur my best coach." In November 2010 Jonathan was sentenced by a judge. Although he was facing a potential verdict of up to ten years in prison for charges of possession of a stolen weapon, evidence against him was weak, and Jonathan was given two years of probation. As he promised me in 2007, he never returned to dealing drugs and weapons, and he has not rejoined a gang.

E-man and Angel periodically stop by our house, most often on a Friday night, unannounced. We talk, catching up on our lives and reminiscing about the past. I hope they remain lifetime friends.

I am clean of cancer. As for the benign and malignant cancerous growths that tried to kill me, my point of view made me a stubborn survivor. And though the little bastards managed to slow me down with some serious detours, I never let them distract me from my journey in life. My attitude allowed me to succeed in baseball and business and beat the odds of succumbing to cancer, while I learned the even tougher lesson that you shouldn't fight alone. You owe it to yourself and others to accept the grace of love.